D1395112

DIRECTING STRATEGY

DIRECTING STRATEGY

The Keys to High Performance

Lloyd S. Baird
Boston University

Alan L. Frohman
Frohman Associates

Prentice Hall, Englewood Cliffs, New Jersey 07632

Library of Congress Cataloging-in-Publication Data

Baird, Lloyd.
    Directing strategy : the keys to high performance / Lloyd S.
Baird, Alan L. Frohman.
        p.   cm.
    ISBN 0-13-220302-2
    1. Industrial management—United States—Case studies.
I. Frohman, Alan L.   II. Title.
HD70.U5B33   1992
658.4'012—dc20   92-6152
                                                      CIP

Acquisitions editor: Garret White
Editorial/production supervision and
    interior design: Brian Hatch
Cover design: Franklyn Graphics
Copy editor: Donna Mulder
Prepress buyer: Trudy Pisciotti
Manufacturing buyer: Robert Anderson

HD
70
·U5
B33
1993

 © 1993 by Prentice-Hall, Inc.
A Simon & Schuster Company
Englewood Cliffs, New Jersey 07632

Printed in the United States of America

10 9 8 7 6 5 4 3 2 1

ISBN 0-13-220302-2

PRENTICE-HALL INTERNATIONAL (UK) LIMITED, *London*
PRENTICE-HALL OF AUSTRALIA PTY. LIMITED, *Sydney*
PRENTICE-HALL CANADA INC., *Toronto*
PRENTICE-HALL HISPANOAMERICANA, S.A., *Mexico*
PRENTICE-HALL OF INDIA PRIVATE LIMITED, *New Delhi*
PRENTICE-HALL OF JAPAN, INC., *Tokyo*
SIMON & SCHUSTER ASIA PTE. LTD., *Singapore*
EDITORA PRENTICE-HALL DO BRASIL, LTDA., *Rio de Janeiro*

*We would like to dedicate this book
to Dorothy Frohman and Bruce Baird*

Contents

Preface

This book is written for practicing managers who have the responsibility of implementing strategy and achieving high performance. It is not about programs and procedures. It is about managerial behaviors you can adopt and is based on the belief that you are the biggest cause of how much your employees are willing to commit, how well they cooperate with each other, how innovative they are, and what they accomplish.

This book is common sense we have gleaned from working with thousands of managers. As we worked with them, we noticed a dramatic difference between the successful and the unsuccessful. The successful managers view their job as working with their people to accomplish organizational results. They view their job as tapping into and releasing the potential that already exists, thereby unleashing high performance. The unsuccessful managers are always looking for more people or at least different people. They always think their problems would be solved by firing, recruiting, and transferring.

Our data base for this book comes from two decades of consulting and research we have done individually and together with corporations ranging in size from large Fortune 100 companies such as Exxon, General Motors, and AT&T to small startup firms with only a few members. In some instances the company or individual is cited by name. In other examples, usually negative, we have used fictitious names and companies for obvious reasons. Fictitious names, when used, are identified as such. Five years ago we began systematically cataloguing our interviews and making comparisons across companies to distill what we observed into usable, practical behaviors. Our five keys to achieving high performance are the results of that synthesis.

We have written the keys so they are easily translated into your job experience. Our intent above all has been to write a book that is to the point and usable. Our best advice is to take the keys and try them—that is the best way to see if they work. At the end of each chapter we provide a list of applications you may find useful. Of course, you can also develop your own.

Many people have helped tremendously in this writing project. Most notably, Mark Frohman and Watt White helped us not only to gather the data and do the interviews, but also to make sense of what we were finding. John Kotter, Chuck Kolb, and Rick Lipsinger were most helpful in their reviews of the initial manuscript. Tanya Phillips, Victoria Selden, Lani Mah, Amy Wentzel, Lisa Horlick, and Judy Park of Boston University all provided the administrative and secretarial support necessary to produce the manuscript. Michelle Poirer often provided the editorial assistance that helped us turn our ideas into thoughts that made sense to others. The Manufacturing Roundtable provided funds that facilitated both the research and the writing. Their financial support, continual critiques of our work, and demands for usefulness have shaped what we have written. We, of course, are responsible for any errors or omissions.

The second author is grateful to others who have helped him along the way. Sandra and David Frohman, my wife and son, provided good common sense and a ready ear whenever either or both were needed. Clients and friends who helped include: John Balboni, John Buono, Gary Dickinson, Marc Fenton, Jim Batchelor, Dick Lacana, Eric Mittelstadt, and Bill Wright.

Lloyd S. Baird
Professor of Management
Boston University

Alan L. Frohman
President
Frohman Associates
Lexington, MA

DIRECTING STRATEGY

CHAPTER 1

Directing Strategy

Recently, the first author attended a performance of *Les Miserables* in Boston. *Les Miserables*, a favorite of mine, is a classic story by Victor Hugo about Jean Valjean, who in his youth is convicted of stealing a loaf of bread. After ten years in prison he is released but because he is a criminal, he cannot get work, nor find a place to stay. A priest befriends him, feeds him, and invites him to stay the night. As he leaves, Jean Valjean steals two silver candlesticks. The police stop him, find the two candlesticks and, convinced he stole them, return him to the priest to verify their charges. The priest greets Jean Valjean as a friend, assures the police he gave the candlesticks as a present, and thanks them for returning Jean Valjean because he forgot to take the two silver plates which were also given as presents. Touched by the priest's kindness, Jean Valjean changes his life, adopts a new identity, and becomes a force for good, helping others. The story has all the elements to create an exceptional experience for the theater audience.

I have read Victor Hugo's book, I have seen the script for the play, and I know the story line. As I went to the performance I was expecting a good experience. Ten minutes into the play I could tell something was happening; this was not going to be a good experience, this was going to be a powerful experience. I started analyzing my own reactions and surveying the audience to see how they were responding. The actors and the audience were like one unit. They ebbed and flowed together. I attributed it to great acting. Then I began comparing it to our discussions about strategy. It was not only great acting, it was a great script writer who provided the words, a great producer who financed and promoted the performance, and a great director who brought it all together on stage to make the audience part of the experience.

Implementing strategy and driving to high performance have the same components. Much attention has been paid by researchers and managers to the writing of strategy. Comparable focus has been given to establishing administrative systems, financial arrangements, and production facilities to implement strategy. What is lacking is an understanding of the manager as the director of strategy. A director who is in the trenches pulling everything together to give customers and organization members an exceptional experience.

For many organizations the strategy is set: reduce cost, increase quality, cut cycle time, increase market share, and be more responsive to customers. The script is already written. But the script is not the performance. The notes on the piece of paper are not the music, and the plan is not the strategy. What is true for plays and concertos is true for strategy—it only exists in the performance.

We believe much can be gained from considering strategy from the viewpoint of a director. Every time *Les Miserables* is performed, Jean Valjean will steal the candlesticks and the priest will forgive him. The difference between the performance of one theater company and another is not the lines of the play. It is how the actors, the staging, the lights, the props, and the audience are brought together to create the experience, and that is the crucial role of the director.

WHAT DO GOOD DIRECTORS DO?

The role of the director is to pull everything together and make the play happen. A hierarchy of activities exists for directors, and the further up the hierarchy they go the better chance they have of delivering an experience to actors and most importantly to the audience.

Level 1: Casting

The director auditions and selects the actors and actresses who will best fit the play. Choices are based on performance ability. After the parts are filled, the director explains to those selected the concept of the play and gives them the script to memorize.

Level 2: Staging

The cast is brought together and begins rehearsal. Rehearsal is a time for the director to work out relationships among characters in the play. The director sets movement on the stage, lighting, music, how lines are delivered, where people stand, and how they relate to each other.

Level 3: Empowering

At a certain point the actors and actresses become their roles. They are no longer repeating memorized lines but the play comes to life. The director is concerned about helping them deliver emotions, feelings, and attitudes, not just lines. The cast goes beyond themselves. The chemistry starts happening, the magic begins. Timing is impeccable, the delivery precise. The play flows. Even into the performance the director is ever present guiding the play. He or she fine tunes and adjusts, constantly improving the experience that is delivered.

The three levels come as building blocks, each built on the foundation of previous levels. Actors must be cast and lines learned before relationships, movements, and timing can be refined. How the play is cast will determine who and what the director has to work with while staging the play.

Likewise, staging provides the framework within which the play is brought to life. The skills actors have and their relationships with others in the play are the raw materials directors use. They are the basis of the audience experience. Once the casting is done and the staging set, the structure of the play is in place. Some may view structure as constraining, but to the competent director, it is freeing. Actors do not have to worry about where others will be standing and what they will be doing. That is established and predictable. They can focus their energy on creating the emotion and the experience. The director does not have to spend his or her time making sure people know their lines and where to stand. He or she can focus on getting the actors to create the experience. Structure provides actors the freedom to perform; the director's job is to help them fill out the roles.

Even though the three levels exist in a building-block relationship, directors may focus on any one of the three. Which they choose will be a consequence of their own style and preference. Some directors focus on casting: Getting the right people in the roles. Some focus on staging: setting lighting and positioning the actors. Some focus on creating the experience. The truly superb directors focus on all three, but they approach them from the perspective of the third. Casting is done to find actors and actresses who can best deliver the experience. The director describes the play to them in terms of the attitudes and feelings of the audience. Staging is done to help the actors and actresses create the emotions. If managers in the role of the director would do the same, the results would be dramatic.

Empowering is a process of setting a clear direction and then helping others go beyond themselves to get there. For both directors and managers, it involves the following keys:

Key #1: Clearly Communicate Strategy
Key #2: Leverage Key Performers

Key #3: Unleash Peoples' Potential
Key #4: Build a Sense of Action and Urgency
Key #5: Continuously Adapt and Improve

By themselves, any one of the keys would have little impact. In fact, some of them in solo would be counterproductive. But enacted together, they create the situation for people to become more than they are. Let us consider each key.

KEY #1: CLEARLY COMMUNICATE STRATEGY

The best scripts are based on core values that are clearly articulated in the words and actions of the actors and actresses. Victor Hugo's book and the play have endured because they are framed around self-sacrifice, humility, and devotion to others. Even if you do not agree with the values, you can admire the clarity with which they are stated and the passion with which they are pursued. The director's job is to help actors and actresses understand the core values, how they are woven into the script, and how their acting will bring the script to life.

As the rehearsals start, the director's first concern is to communicate his or her concept of the play. The director communicates to the cast in terms of feelings and emotions he or she wants the audience to experience. The director explains what the script is saying and the message to be delivered. During rehearsals and on into performances of the play, the director will constantly bring actors and actresses back to the concept, "Remember what we are trying to say here."

Once the core values and message of the play are explained, the actors and actresses have to go through a process of adoption. They have to learn their lines, let them seep in to the point the words become their own, and put on the mask of the character. What was surprising to hear in talking to actors and directors was how little they talked about learning their lines. They simply accepted the need to learn their lines; they spent their time worrying about who the character really was and how they would act and react. They went much deeper than memorizing words in a script. They became the role.

Directors of strategy have the same challenge. Employees must understand the core values and feel the strategy so deeply that they become that strategy. Communicating the strategy goes far beyond giving employees a written copy. Employees have to adopt the strategy, they have to learn it, letting it seep in to the point where it becomes their own.

Figure 1–1 represents data from a division of a major U.S. manufacturer showing how hard it is to communicate strategy to the point of adoption. This firm's stated strategy is to reduce costs to deliver more customer value and improve its competitive position. Presently, this firm's costs are

FIGURE 1-1 ▪ Understanding Competitive Position

Question: What is our competitive position in the world market?

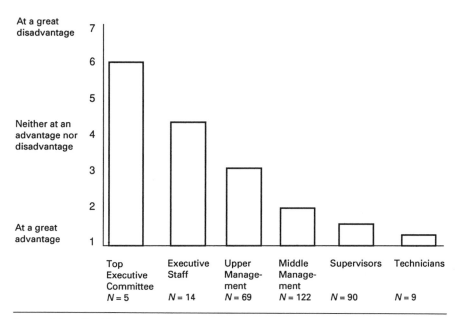

Source of data: Used by permission from *Strategy Action Questionnaire* (Frohman Associates, Lexington, MA).

23 percent higher than competitors. To survive it must become cost competitive. The company's executives have made speeches. Statistics and graphs are published in the company's newsletters. The business plan includes objectives for reducing the competitive disadvantage. Yet the further down into the organization, the less employees understand, accept, and are committed to the organization strategy. The bulk of organization is oblivious to the problems it faces. The problem in this, as well as in many organizations, is management assumes all it needs to do is hand employees the script and assign them their roles.

Keep Strategy Simple

Simplicity is the key to successful communicating strategy. Employees can spend their time figuring out how to bring a strategy to life rather than trying to figure out what it is. If employees cannot repeat the strategy after hearing it once, it is too complex. If they cannot remember it after reading it, the strategy is too long. Einstein once said, "The elegance of a good theory is its simplicity in use." The same applies to strategy.

The Pontiac Motor Division of General Motors provides a good example of the power of simplicity. When Bill Hoglund took over as head, the

Pontiac Division was losing market share. They had lost their sense of focus and purpose. Hoglund was given the mandate to turn it around. What Pontiac needed was a purpose. He called the Pontiac employees together and charged them with the responsibility of developing a unifying theme for the division. His only instructions were to keep it simple, keep it memorable, keep it focused. This effort resulted in the Pontiac strategy statement, "We build excitement," a theme that has steadily increased market share. In 1988 this strategy resulted in *Car and Driver* naming the Pontiac Grand Prix car of the year. This is the strategy that energizes, integrates, and coordinates the Pontiac units. It is the basis for their car designs. It serves as the theme for their advertising. It serves as the common bond among all units in the Pontiac Division. Across the door of an engineering design control group, a large sign written in computer graphics reads: "We monitor excitement." That is when Hoglund knew he had made it. The strategy had permeated the organization to such an extent that it affected what people thought and how they acted on a daily basis.

Use Multiple Channels to Communicate

Repeat, repeat, repeat. Think about how actors rehearse. They go over and over the same parts. The directors keep reminding them what they are trying to accomplish. The manager must do the same. Weave the strategy into speeches, presentations, interviews, discussions, meetings, reward systems, plans, anywhere you can get it in. You may tire of saying the same thing over and over, but the people listening will not tire of hearing the same thing. They will start believing you when everything you do and say communicates the strategy.

For example, Mark Abbott, as head of Polysar's Latex Division, invited all of the top management group together for a kick-off dinner after a new business strategy was developed. The dinner was held on a large glass covered table. Under the glass at each manager's place in bold print was the portion of the business strategy for which each was responsible. As they ate and talked the next two hours, their personal responsibilities stared them in the face. Even if it spoiled a few appetites, it drove the point home. The strategy was visibly stated in terms appropriate for each unit; for example, growth in the market segment a unit served, or profitability for the area a manager controlled.

Executives have a host of formal activities during which they may reinforce strategy. Retirement parties, speeches to community groups, presentations at management meetings, and speeches to employee groups are but a handful of examples. A good test of your effectiveness at formal activities is the extent to which you can double dip, in other words, do more than one thing at a time. For example, to ingrain the Pontiac strategy, "We build excitement," into the working life of employees, Bill Hoglund used every opportunity to repeat the theme. Numerous formal occasions, plant startups, retirement parties, executive meetings, and conferences all became opportunities to repeat and explain the strategy.

KEY #2: LEVERAGE KEY PERFORMERS

Every play has key roles. It may be the stars or it may be a supporting role that carries the theme of the play. Often it will be two or three key roles playing off each other to set up the drama, create the problem to be solved, or establish the comical situation. The director's job is to identify the key roles, build the actors' competence to perform them, and leverage their performance.

Key roles in a play are determined by the flow of the play. For example, in the beginning of plays, a great deal of information has to be provided to set the scheme, introduce the characters, and establish the conflict, dilemma, or issue serving as the basis of the play. Key roles are those which can very efficiently provide that information. Later on, as intrigue or comedy builds, key roles may shift to someone who provides new insight or conflict in the play. In plays, the nature of the script determines the key roles. Most importantly, though, the nature of the experience the director wants to deliver also determines the key roles and how they must be performed. In the play *Les Miserables*, Jean Valjean conceals his identity and gradually rises to positions of wealth and influence, eventually becoming mayor of Montreuil-sur-mer. One day he finds a crowd beating a woman, Fantine. He saves her from the mob and has her cared for in the infirmary. As she lies feverish and dying her only concern is Cosette, her daughter. As Jean Valjean cares for Fantine, he begins a life-long devotion to Cosette. The role of Fantine can be played many ways but if the audience is to be drawn into Jean Valjean's continuing sacrifice for Cosette, they must feel his sense of identification and commitment to Fantine. They must despair with the woman's loss and they must sense the vulnerability of Cosette.

Although the role of the woman is not lengthy, it is one of the pivotal points determining whether the audience gets a good experience or a great experience. Organizations also have key pivotal points on which success rests. If activities from these performers fail to produce the proper results, the total organization fails. If they succeed, they provide a basis for the rest of the organization. Consider the following.

Understanding what the customer wants is crucial if a company is to be market driven. Customers have needs and they are searching for products that come closest to filling those needs. The customer defines what shades of blues and reds are important in the pictures they take, not the research scientist developing film. A pivotal role for a market-driven company interested in selling photographic film is someone who can define what the customer wants in terms of product specifications and then drive those specifications into product characteristics. In a research environment the critical role belongs to scientists. Without their discoveries nothing can be done. In a soft-drink firm the core roles are in distribution, with those in advertising following a close second. The motto in the soft-drink industry is "within an arm's length of desire." They want to get the soft drink as close to customers as possible, knowing customers will likely drink whatever is most readily available. Those who manage the distribution network in a soft-drink firm will drive the rest of the decisions.

The nature of the cosmetics industry is best summarized by the motto, "In the factory we make perfume and in the store we sell hope." The key roles that leverage what others do are in advertising and marketing. The image must be created before anything can be sold. Key performers are not defined by rank or credentials. In organizations pivotal roles are defined by the strategy, just as pivotal roles in plays are defined by the script. As the strategy changes, the key roles change. When creating a new product or service, research and development is key. After the product is developed, market share must be obtained and production costs driven down. Key roles shift to production and marketing. In a declining market those best positioned to manage costs and cutbacks become key. Even within one project the key roles will shift over time. At the startup, those who can clearly define the task and set the priorities are critical. At other times, those who manage the decision-making process are critical. To effectively direct strategy, managers must be able to sense when each role is important and direct the ebb and flow of the key roles, just as the director does in the play.

After the key roles are identified, the next step is getting the right people to fill them. Directors cast plays and so must managers. There is no magic involved—both managers and directors must hire, train, and reward to get the right people in the right positions.

The third step, leveraging key performers, is most critical. They must affect much more than just the performance on their own job. They must affect what other people do. A common statement made about truly great actors and actresses is that when they are on the stage, everybody's performance improves. The same must be true of key performers. Much of the leveraging will happen because of their individual skills, but some can be built into their jobs. Key performers should be placed in visible situations, key task forces, important presentations, and in critical decision points in a project's life. Only if they are able to affect the work of many will their true potential be realized.

KEY #3: UNLEASH PEOPLES' POTENTIAL

Truly great directors help actors realize their potential and go beyond. They take what has been described as the Michelangelo approach to directing. Michelangelo viewed his job as a sculptor as releasing the figure that already existed in the stone. He simply had to chip away the stone that was not the figure. Lesser artists view their job as creating the figure. Directors spend considerable time and energy understanding the actors and how they work. They get them to go beyond where they have never gone before, giving the performance of a lifetime. Most actors come to a play with far more potential than they use. The director's job is to remove the constraints they put on themselves and release their natural ability. It is not a creating job; directors cannot create what is not there. It is an unleashing job.

We find in many situations the problem of energizing people is not a creation problem, not a question of bringing in new people, but it is an unleashing problem, that is, determining how to cut back constraints so people can perform. Management's main questions to employees become:

- "What can I do to help you do your job more effectively?"
- "What can I do to reduce the time you waste?"
- "What can we take care of for you so that you can focus on your job?"

Most people have far more potential than they use on their jobs. Systems, procedures, and managers get in their way. The Peter Principle reinforces this way of thinking.

In 1965, Laurence Peter formulated what become known as the Peter Principle to explain many problems in organizations.[1] The Peter Principle proposed that people are promoted based on their ability to do their current job. They will be promoted until they reach a job they cannot do. There they remain; that is, people rise to the level of their incompetence.

Because everyone eventually rises to the level of their incompetence, organizations are staffed by people who cannot do their jobs. Fortunately, great directors do not believe the Peter Principle, nor should managers.

Although it gives managers a simplistic explanation of organization problems, several fallacies exist in the Peter Principle. It assumes people have a limit to their energy and ability. They will advance until they hit their limit and then stop striving. Having hit the limit, they will be content to accept their own low level of incompetence, with the rationalization that the job is beyond them.

Also inherent in the Peter Principle is a focus on making decisions based on present performance rather than on potential and future performance. The present is what counts. Get the product out the door now. If workers are not performing, accept their level of incompetence and work around them. If workers are performing, use them. This orientation causes problems. First, promotions and other management decisions are always based on ability to do past and present jobs, not ability to do future jobs. With this orientation, many organizations promote very good technicians

---

[1]Laurence J. Peter, *The Peter Principle* (New York: William Morrow, 1972), p. 11.

to be very bad managers. Second, workers do not have expectations that developing and improving is part of the present job. Third, managers do not receive any recognition for developing people unless it contributes to the immediate task.

We are not arguing that present performance should be ignored; it cannot be ignored. We are arguing that both present and future performance must be managed simultaneously. Figure 1-2 lists performance measures for managing both present and future performance. The measures of present performance are important because they are the basis for day-to-day judgments. However, without the measure of future performance in the second column, managers are rewarded solely for consuming resources and producing short-term results, not building and preparing for the future.

FIGURE 1-2 ▪ Managing Present and Future Performance

Present Performance	Future Performance
Short-term results	Long-term results
Resource consumption	Resources developed
Skills	Ability to learn and adapt
Knowledge	Ability to coach and develop others

The assumptions that people continually learn, and that management's job is to manage future and potential performance as well as present performance can provide substantial payoff to the organization. The level of present performance increases because each person is motivated to do the job as it exists, to solve problems and look for better ways to do the jobs and prepare for the challenges they will face in the future. Future performance also increases because employees are constantly striving to improve and prepare for the future. Directors and managers are alike—the great ones get ordinary people to give extraordinary performances.

KEY #4: BUILD A SENSE OF ACTION AND URGENCY

Directors must build the excitement of the cast for what they are doing. The critics' reviews, the audiences' applause, and the spotlights all help, but even so, the energy of the actors ebbs and flows. Some days actors are up; other days they are down. That is human nature, but the director cannot let it translate into a low performance. A great director knows how to build and sustain excitement so that the 350th performance of *Les Miserables* comes off better than the first.

Directors do this by holding cast parties to celebrate reviews, continually involving the cast in improving the play, structuring press meetings, drama club reviews, and other occasions so the cast continues to receive feedback and opportunities to review the results of their work. Managers must do the same.

Focus on a Limited Number of Surmountable Factors

Mangers can successfully energize employees to purposeful action by focusing on a limited number of surmountable factors. Nobody can do everything, so focus on those factors that promise maximum payoff. Major problems will usually have to be tackled in parts; therefore, as a first step, tackle the most significant piece. Take the biggest bite you can. Once it has been digested, take another bite. Solve each part of the problem and move on. As the riddle wisely phrased it: How do you eat an elephant? One bite at a time.

There are two requirements for this approach. First, focus on the most crucial issues, those central to the organization's growth and survival. If your product or service isn't selling well, identify the reason. What competitive advantage do you lack? Is price too high, quality poor, service unreliable, advertising ineffective? Do not do something just because it is easy to do. Do it because an analysis of the problem identifies it as the crucial element.

Second, focus on factors you control. You are not omnipotent. For example, Aerodyne Research, Inc., whose business was mainly with the U.S. government, found it could not compete with the larger firms for the quantity of talented people it desperately needed. The company simply could not recruit experienced people. They typically had established homes and families and were unwilling to move. Larger firms not only offered better compensation packages, they also had greater financial resources to spend on recruiting.

Aerodyne's financial disadvantage in relation to the larger firms was something they could not control. Their recruitment strategy, however, they could control. Working diligently through contacts in the academic community, they established consulting contracts with professors who had the background they were after. The professors provided the top-level talent, as well as the graduate students, to help do the work. As a positive side effect, the students gained practical experience and access to job opportunities. Several took jobs with Aerodyne after graduating because they were familiar with the projects and enjoyed working with the company. Aerodyne had circumvented an uncontrollable factor and designed a creative, effective way to handle staffing shortages.

Celebrate the Small Victories and Early Wins

To maintain the energy you create, celebrate the small victories and early wins. People need to see signs of progress, they need reassurance something is happening. After opening night, the director hosts a cast party; the next day everyone reads the press reviews. Business managers must do the same. Do not wait until the end of the period or the next planning cycle to let people know how they are doing. Get them plugged into success as quickly as possible.

In fact, it is best to design the program or project so a few early wins are guaranteed. Do not wait until the full objective is accomplished to celebrate. People will tire. They need encouragement and a sense that progress is being made. Small celebrations let them know their efforts are paying off. Of course, if the reviews are terrible, good directors let the cast know they are terrible. Actors and employees can only improve if they have accurate information.

Recently, Aerodyne suffered a very difficult year. Dramatic actions were taken to cut expenses. The following year management set ambitious sales targets to pull themselves out of the hole. Each time a contract was signed, they celebrated with an ice cream party. Not fancy or expensive, but a recognizable celebration. It worked to keep the people enthusiastic. They felt like heros, rather than losers crawling out of the cellar.

We use the word *celebrate* deliberately. Ceremony is necessary. It does not have to be formal, but it must be visible. Ceremonies accomplish four things simultaneously: they recognize those who are achieving; they are sign posts identifying progress; they keep people up to date and give them the feeling that they are in that inner circle making things happen; and they provide a chance for managers to clarify the strategy.

Celebrate the win as soon after it happens as possible. The ceremony can take many forms: A special recognition at a staff meeting, a dinner, a party, or a presentation in the noted person's area. These early celebrations need little planning or preparation, since visibility is the critical ingredient. Save the big, formal celebration for when the project is completed.

Make Sure Everyone Understands the Competition

A good way to build a sense of action and urgency is to make sure everyone understands the competition. Competition has increased dramatically in every sector of the economy over the last ten years. Not only has general productivity increased, but deregulation and internationalization have introduced competitors not even in existence ten years ago.

The purpose of competitive analysis is to familiarize your people with what others are doing. Competitive analysis and taking the necessary action to be competitive should be part of everyone's job. Planning should include competitive analysis and actions. A proposal for a new product or service should include an analysis of competitive products. Decisions about new production processes should include a competitive analysis. Wage and salary decisions should be based on competitive analysis. In short, part of everyone's responsibility should be understanding how they compare to others outside of the organization, and to take action to ensure competitiveness.

KEY #5: CONTINUOUSLY ADAPT AND IMPROVE

After all the communicating, building competence, leveraging, and unleashing, potential managers are often tempted to sit back and watch the results of their work. After all, delegation means turning responsibility over to the actors and letting them perform. That does not work for directors and it does not work for managers. The director's job is never done: Actors get tired; audiences change; new ideas are developed; reviewers give useful comments; new plays open next door; things happen in the economy and society that affect both the actors and the audience. Good directors are constantly refining, refining, refining.

Unfortunately, there will be no rest in business either. The simple fact is that you will not get it right the first time. You will have to continuously adapt and improve. Not because you have not given it your best efforts, but because the situation is not stable and the game is never over.

Many mangers want to believe the situation is stable and they can anticipate what is going to happen. Their job, they feel, is to solve one crisis at a time, each as it arises. They feel comfortable identifying a critical problem, determining a solution, managing the implementation process, and then moving on to the next problem. Many of our management systems reinforce this focus on one objective at a time. Planning systems are designed to identify the objective. Monitoring, control, and performance appraisal systems are established to evaluate progress toward the objective. We want to believe the world only changes after the objective is accomplished. This just isn't the case, as giants such as IBM, GM, and Xerox who saw their once unassailable leads evaporate can testify. Managers must direct so performance is always improving.

A fascinating example of the dangers of assuming the world is stable is the custom of "product tear down." As sometimes practiced in American industry, the custom of product tear down involves buying competitors' products, tearing them down to see how they are made, and then building an equal or superior product. For example, American car manufacturers buy cars made by Honda, Toyota, Mercedes-Benz, and other competitors, take them apart, and identify product characteristics that should be included in American cars. They then develop engineering designs and production plans to produce a hybrid of "the best of the best."

Assuming it takes four years to go from designing to saleable product, four years from now American cars will be perfectly designed to compete with this year's Hondas, Toyotas, and Mercedes. And the American cars will of course still be three years behind their competitors. Managers in all organizations are shooting at a moving target and they must constantly adapt and improve.

Most people want to improve and do better. None of us get out of bed in the morning saying "I want to do worse today." Often we are forced to do worse because information is not presented so we can do better. Performers on stage receive a great deal of feedback from audiences and critics. This is not often the case for most employees. Feedback is infrequent and their performance is often not visible. Managers have a job much more difficult than the director: Building the systems to enable employees to monitor performance.

Most current systems do not provide the data employees need to monitor and adapt. Accounting and budgeting systems provide financial data too aggregated and too late for individual workers trying to improve. Managers must get their people the data they need.

Make the Data Directly Relevant
to Employee Responsibilities

Employees pay attention to data about what they are responsible for and can control. General data on overall corporate performance must be broken down so employees receive information that is specifically relevant to their performance. One effective way to ensure data are relevant is to have employees collect these data themselves. They know what they need. Make employees responsible for tracking their success and their contributions to performance.

Monitor the Critical Issues

The second requirement for monitoring to drive continuous improvement is that it focuses on priority concerns. The most rigorous assessments are meaningless if the measures do not relate to what is important. In some cases the analysts become tied up in their own data by going to great lengths to provide quotes, numbers, or charts. We find managers have a very limited interest in excessive amounts of data. They will only maintain interest in a report that helps them improve performance.

Aim at the Right Level

Monitoring the implementation of strategy can be a valuable spur to action. But for this to happen, information needs to go to the people who have the power to act on it. If information goes to a level above where it is needed, then employees feel managers are looking over their shoulders. The game is no longer monitoring and improving, it is justifying yourself to the boss. If information goes to a level below where it is needed, the employee who needs it never gets it and is powerless to act. Information concerning whether defects are high, turnover is high, or attitudes are not positive must go to decision makers who can do something about these problems. Managers must be able to take ownership of the problem and take action. If relevant data do not go to the decision makers who can use it, nothing will get done.

CONCLUSION

The world of the theatre has long recognized the importance of great directors. Organizations must now do the same. All employees are directors. For many organizations, the script is written and the stage set. All that remains is the keen eye and steady guidance of a competent director to bring strategy to life. The challenge is to make sure employees clearly understand their role in making strategy happen and help them go beyond what they perceive as their natural limits. In Chapter 2 we lay out the value base of the five keys to high performance. As with good strategy, the keys are value driven. In subsequent chapters, we discuss each of the keys and provide examples of how they are used in organizations.

CHAPTER **2**

The Value Bases
of Action

B y now some of you are nodding your heads and saying, yes of course
those are sound keys for high performance and they describe how I
manage. For some, these keys will sound immediately right. They support
your biases. You see the world a certain way and our keys fit your way of
managing. You will go on reading hoping we have some new techniques
you might use. We do, and you should enjoy reading about our experiences.

Some might not agree with us. Our keys may not sound like they will
work. They may not match your experiences and biases. You are willing to
give us a little more time, but so far you are not getting much help. Let us
suggest we are both right. While from our perspective our keys work, from
your perspective they may not make sense. It is the perspectives that make
the difference. The keys provide the maximum payoff if adopted from the
proper perspective. Their usefulness is limited if they do not match your
assumptions about people and the nature of work. To understand and use
them to maximum advantage you need to understand the perspective from
which they have been developed, the values that serve as the bases for the
keys to high performance.

In this chapter we lay out our own perspectives and assumptions
which create the foundation for our discussions of high performance. We
also show you how our values differ from others. Once you understand
our values, the keys follow rather easily.

THE VALUE BASES OF ACTION

We each have essential values which affect our assumptions about people and work, and establish our base of action. Our values determine the perspectives we take when dealing with problems and frame our decisions and actions. We have known for a long time that people's values and perspectives differ. Perhaps the best-known references of how different perspectives affect action in management come from the writings of March and Simon, who talk about how people limit the amount of information they use.[1] We can all absorb only so much. We have certain lenses through which we see the world. These lenses filter out information and help us make sense of what is happening around us. As a consequence, we each see the world differently. Faced with the same set of realities, we each react in our own way.

For simplicity of discussion, we have identified three different bases of action from which managers can operate: control, exchange, and empowerment. Let us look carefully at how each affects managers' views of the world and how they respond to situations. Figure 2–1 summarizes our discussion.

Control

Managers whose value base is predominantly control see their main activities as making sure tasks go according to plans and procedures, setting objectives, and controlling action. They use policies, procedures, standards, and plans as the main focus. They take these as doctrine and use them to focus time, effort, and energy. The main concern of a control-oriented person is that tasks are done on time and by the rules. Deviations from prescribed performance are seen as bad and conformance as good. Progress is measured in terms of deviation from the standard, plan, or objective. Obedience is the most important human characteristic. The dominant managerial question is "How can *I* get *you* to help me accomplish *my* objective?" Failure happens when *we* do not accomplish *my* objective.

Exchange

Exchange-oriented managers are concerned with contracts and exchanges in relationships. Costs and benefits must be balanced. Equity is critical. As managers, their main activity is negotiating and managing relationships. Attention is focused on enforcement of contracts. Difficulties are resolved by negotiation. They are concerned with achieving satisfactory relation-

---

[1]James G. March and Herbert A. Simon, *Organizations* (New York: John Wiley & Sons, Inc., 1958).

FIGURE 2-1 ▪ Bases of Action

Base	Dominant Concern	Use of Information	Performance Orientation	Response to Failure
Control	We accomplish my objectives	Monitor deviations from standard	Accomplish predefined objectives	Eliminate deviations
Exchange	We accomplish our objectives	Monitor relationships	Enforce contracts	Enforce, renegotiate, cancel
Empowerment	I accomplish my objective by helping you accomplish your objective	Self-management learning	Remove barriers, assist development	Adjust, change

ships based on equity and fairness. Their main use of information is for establishing contracts, reasoning together, arbitration, and negotiation to determine what is appropriate. Rewards and punishments are determined by the contract. Fairness is a dominant concern. The exchange works if both parties get what the contract specifies. What is right to exchange-oriented managers is a fair day's work for a fair day's pay—that the costs and benefits for the manager and employee balance out. The dominant managerial orientation is structuring deals so *we* both accomplish *our* objectives. The dominant managerial question is "How can *we* work together so *you* can accomplish *your* objectives and *I* can accomplish *mine?*" Failure happens when the contract is not upheld.

Empowerment

Those with a core value of empowerment are concerned with innovation, development, change, and unleashing potential. Control is accomplished not by imposing restraints but by building intrinsic control mechanisms into the work situation and holding the worker responsible for self-control. Rewards and punishments are also often intrinsic. Failure is considered to be a learning opportunity. Managers focus on helping employees perform. Criteria for success are innovation, change, adaptability, and growth. The dominant managerial orientation is helping. Managers and employees work hard to establish compatible objectives; *I* accomplish *my* objective by helping *you* accomplish *yours.* Failure happens when *we* fail to innovate, change, and adapt.

TAKING ACTION

We find most managers use one of these bases of action more than the other two. Our base of action frames what we do to such an extent that we respond differently to the same situation. For example, an emphasis on quality can be approached from any of the three perspectives. A manufacturing manager we know, whose dominant value base is control, looked at the pressure for quality coming from his company and saw it as an opportunity to set clear goals and establish a new set of measurements, rewards, and punishments for achieving those goals.

A second manufacturing manager saw the emphasis on quality as an opportunity to renegotiate with workers a new set of quality objectives they should strive for, how they were going to try to reach them, and by when. He established what he called "quality contracts" that specified what was to be the improvement in quality over the course of the year.

A third manager, who is more empowerment oriented, used the quality thrust as an opportunity to share with his workers the company's competitive challenge, why the company was behind the competition, and what the performance of the competition was in terms of quality. He then brought the workers together and helped them hammer out quality objectives for all to work toward, and the budget necessary to reach those goals.

Differences in these three orientations will be most manifest in a person's performance orientation, use of information, and response to failure.

Performance Orientation

Managers' value orientations frame their concerns about performance, what they monitor, and what they define as success. Those with a control orientation are concerned about accomplishing their predefined objectives. They monitor progress toward the goal and measure performance in terms of fixed standards. They evaluate employees in terms of compliance and accomplishment of predefined objectives. Their main concern is regulating activities within acceptable boundaries.

Those with an exchange orientation are concerned with maintaining relationships. For them, success is determined by the willingness of parties to cooperate and become engaged in exchanges. Their main performance concern is follow-through: Accomplishing what they said they would, holding up their end of the bargain, and ensuring that the other parties to the contract hold up their end.

From an empowerment perspective, the manager is concerned about facilitating his or her employees' ability to perform, innovate, and revitalize the organization. The concerns are growth, adaptation, fit, and responsiveness. The focus is on constantly improving not only the way work is performed but what is done. The empowerment-oriented manager worries not only about "doing things right" but also about "doing the right things."

Use of Information

The performance orientation determines the type of data needed. From a control perspective, information is used to monitor deviations from fixed standards. Information becomes the basis for regulating activities and adjusting performance.

From an exchange perspective, information is the basis for monitoring the relationship and enforcing the negotiated contracts.

From an empowerment perspective, information is the basis for self-management and learning. The individual becomes responsible for collecting, synthesizing, and using information to identify and solve performance problems, and constantly looks for new and better strategies. The dominant concerns are adapting to the environment, innovating, responding, and growing.

Response to Failure

The clearest indication of a manager's value base is how he or she responds to failure. Because the main concern from a control orientation is performance within guidelines, failure is defined as deviations from the guidelines. Failure is dealt with by attempting to eliminate deviations. Typically, fixed procedures are already established, contingency plans outlined, and reactions specified if performance falls outside of what is accepted.

Failure in an exchange orientation happens when contracts are broken or exchanges are not carried out as agreed. Equity is not maintained, just rewards and punishments are not given. Failure is dealt with by enforcing, renegotiating, or perhaps even cancelling the contract. Sometimes a new cost-benefit structure is established so new relationships can be formed. New methods of relating and exchanging are established.

From an empowerment perspective, failure happens when efforts do not produce results that fit the demands of the situation and individuals fail to learn, adjust, and change to fit. Failures occur when people learn nothing and make no attempt to either change themselves so they do fit the situation, or move themselves to a situation in which they will be successful. Managers deal with this type of failure by helping the individual adjust or changing the situation so a fit exists. If neither works, the person is moved to a new situation.

Not only do managers react to failure differently depending on their orientation, but they also design information systems and organization structures to help them maintain their orientation. For example, managers with a control orientation will design systems through which they can compare costs against budgets to identify variances. Those with an exchange orientation will develop and implement systems to compare costs and benefits. They will also be particularly concerned with how they stack up against competition. Managers with an empowerment orientation will develop systems to constantly define and refine the strategic objective. They will put in place information and systems to help them constantly reassess what they are doing and accomplishing within the context of shifting environments.

What We See Depends on Where We Sit

Each base of action frames how we see others. In general, we like those who share our values and perspectives. A manager operating from a control base will see other control-oriented managers as efficient, focused, and able to accomplish the task. He or she will see exchange-oriented managers as tedious in their negotiations and spending far too much time worrying about whether people are treated fairly. Empowering managers are seen as abdicating responsibility: Passive and weak, not stating the rules or enforcing what needs to be done.

Those operating from a control base are no more biased than others operating from different bases, they just have a different orientation. Managers whose base of action is exchange, view control-oriented managers as unfair and arbitrary. These managers state rules, policies, and procedures and do not provide enough opportunity for negotiation or give-and-take. Managers who seek to empower employees are seen as manipulating employees to get the most out of them, without stating in advance the rewards for a job well done.

Likewise, empowerment-oriented managers view control-oriented managers as overbearing and punishing. They also view the negotiations, contracts, and focus on relationships of the person concerned with exchange as bureaucratic and legalistic.

In truth, we all overemphasize the contribution and advantages of our preferred action base and underemphasize the contribution and benefits of others. We are like the vain queen in *Snow White* who looks into the mirror and asks, "Mirror, mirror on the wall, who is the fairest of them all?" We too tend to look in mirrors for answers to determine the best way of managing.

THE VALUE BASE
OF HIGH PERFORMANCE

Our value biases are probably apparent from the discussion so far, but let us make them clear. We believe the world of work is changing dramatically. Explosive developments in technology, the rapid shifts in information systems, globalization, and increased competition are combining to create a very complex work environment, where the rate of change is unprecedented.

We are not alone in arguing that these shifts will have dramatic implications for the practice and tools of management. Drucker, for example, describes a shift from control-based to information-based organizations largely devoid of middle-level management.[2] Knowledge to make informed business decisions will reside primarily at the bottom of the organization in the hands of specialists who direct their own work. Information will be used for self-guidance, not top-down control. There will be a greater reliance on self-discipline and individual responsibility.

In a recent best seller, Shoshana Zuboff argues that technology will redefine our work lives.[3] Adding to or changing the technology of the organization is not, and should not be, viewed as incremental adjustments, replacing human judgment with computer intelligence and increas-

---

[2]Peter Drucker, "The Coming of the New Organization," *Harvard Business Review*, 88, no. 1 (January-February 1988), 45–53.

[3]Shoshana Zuboff, *In the Age of the Smart Machine* (New York: Basic Books, Inc., 1988).

ing management's ability to control organization members. Rather, technology can be used to transform the nature of work and help employees realize their full potential. Relationships between managers and employees will be more intricate, collaborative, and bound by mutual responsibility. Hierarchical distinctions will blur. Authority will depend more on knowledge than on hierarchical position. As technology integrates information across organizational units, managers and employees will have an opportunity to overcome their narrow unit focus and adopt an overriding concern for the customer.

When combined, these forces create organizations where information and responsibility are thrust downward. Change comes rapidly and people must constantly adapt and learn. If managers and organizations are to be successful, authority and accountability must also be thrust downward. Employees must be empowered to make decisions and adjust to ever-changing realities.

The frames of reference or value bases from which most managers operate will limit or enhance performance in this new reality. They limit performance by constraining what employees are willing and able to do. If the dominant orientation of management is control, the dominant response of employees is keeping their noses clean, doing what they are asked to do, keeping on target, and accomplishing the plan. That may sound good to many managers, and to a point, it is. The problem is that employees do only what they are asked and then stop, waiting for the next direction. Self-initiation, problem solving, and innovation will be missing.

If the dominant orientation of management is exchange, the dominant response of employees is negotiation—what is in it for me? The goal becomes important if it leads to rewards. Inordinate amounts of time are spent negotiating, establishing rewards and punishments, and resolving inequities—time that could be spent producing. Because situations are never clear and always changing, relationships must always be renegotiated, eating up even more productive time.

If the dominant orientation of management is empowerment, the dominant response of employees is involvement, innovation, change, and creativity. The objective becomes not only doing the job as defined, but figuring out how it can be done better and what else should be done. The concern is changing and adapting as the situation changes.

The Steps Forward

While we believe an empowerment value base best fits the nature of work and the environment we all face, we do not discount the importance of control and exchange. By empowerment we do not mean letting everyone do whatever they want. Empowerment is built on a foundation of control. Employees are given freedom to produce and are held responsible for results. Employees managed from an empowerment base must understand goals, budgets, control, and monitoring perhaps even better than those managed from a different action base, because they are responsible for self-control. True empowerment cannot happen until workers fully understand the basis of control. Likewise, empowerment is built on exchange. Natural consequences exist for actions taken and not taken. Relationships and dependencies on others must be clearly understood. Cost and benefits must be calculated to make proper choices.

Control and exchange are the building blocks on which true empowerment is constructed. If they are not in place, the self-management, change, and innovation of empowerment will lead to chaos. Our challenge then in developing these keys for high performance was to develop a set which empowers workers to purposeful, focused, productive action. If your orientation is control, these keys will increase your control by clarifying direction and involving more of your employees' skills and energy in accomplishing meaningful objectives. If your orientation is exchange, these keys clarify roles and responsibilities and make working together easier. Most importantly, these keys will help both the control-oriented and exchange-oriented manager begin to direct strategy from a base of empowerment and begin to create a powerful experience for employees.

In the next chapter, we discuss the first key to high performance, clearly communicating strategy. Without a clear understanding of strategy, employees have no target for performance. Succeeding chapters then provide detailed discussions of each of the remaining four keys. No one key leads to high performance. They must all be used simultaneously.

CHAPTER 3

Key #1: Clearly Communicate Strategy

A merican autos, steel, machinery, and other industries have for some time been at a cost disadvantage when compared to Japanese, South Korean, and other foreign manufacturers. For example, to produce a comparable car it costs the American producer an average of $500 to $1,000 more than foreign competitors. This is not an industry secret. It is reported in trade journals, it is graphically presented in speeches, it is included in business plans. What needs to be done is quite clear: Deliver customer satisfaction and simultaneously reduce the cost of making a car. Competitors have done it by staying linked to the consumer, controlling labor and resource costs, driving efficient operations, simplifying design, and improving organization efficiency. Why can't we? We repeatedly find one key reason: few middle-level managers, technicians, secretaries, assembly-line workers, and engineers in these industries understand the magnitude of the challenge they face. These people are the "guts" of the organization. They do the work which determines organization success or failure. Business has many words to describe what needs to be done: mission, strategy, objectives, and goals. No matter which one you use, the simple fact is that if employees do not understand the core values and key objectives of the organization, they are not very likely to accomplish them.

Many organizations face the problem of employees who do not understand what needs to be done; they do not understand the company's or unit's strategy. Managers throughout industry wonder in frustration, "I told them, what is the problem?" Telling employees your strategy in one or two rousing speeches is not enough for them to understand and accept the strategy. It must be repeated often. It must be reinforced through plans, reward systems, speeches, presentations, meetings, through everything employees do. Rephrase it, paraphrase it, create symbols of it, do anything to keep reminding people what is to be accomplished. Let us look first at why it is so hard for employees to understand and then at what you can do to get the message across.

WHY DON'T PEOPLE UNDERSTAND?

Why don't people understand? They do not "understand" because managers' actions do not consistently fit the message. And without consistency there is no strategy. Managers do not pick a focus and stick to it. The walk does not fit the talk. The following is a quote from an employee in the packaging division of a consumer products firm.

> We tried that same quality strategy in '75, '79, and '86. Each time it lasted for a few months then, regardless of what management says, they always go back to the same old stuff. The emphasis on quality usually only lasts a couple of months and then just like the tide, it goes out. If you stick around long enough you get used to ignoring what management says. We have seen all of this before. There is no long lasting strategy except the strategy of personal survival.

Employees do not implement the new program because they do not believe management is serious. The organization landscape is littered with fits and starts, new thrusts and programs never pushed to completion or payoff. Managers sometimes try to cloak the fits and starts in a blanket of market responsiveness, reading the market and being able to adjust quickly. Employees see it as managers not knowing what they are doing. Fits and starts are a way of organizational life, but if employees cannot pick up the pattern of a new strategy, they cannot properly direct their energies.

Advanced Systems (a fictitious name) is a developer of electronic equipment in New England. It is heavily dependent on government contracts. For the last 15 years Advanced Systems had a stated strategy of diversifying into the industrial sector. Whenever business slows in the government sector, the company mounts a program to capture business from industry. They pursue industrial contracts until new government contracts arrive. Then they abandon the industrial strategy until government business is slow again. Over the years it has become more and more difficult to convince employees that the company is serious about developing industrial business. Employees will have a hard time accepting a new direction when all the systems, procedures, structures, and in fact their own skills are repeatedly refocused to the old direction. They do not hear the new because the old is ringing so loudly in their ears. Is it any wonder employees question whether management even has a strategy?

Many organizations have attempted to introduce quality improvement programs, and have learned firsthand what happens if the walk does not fit the talk. One example is a manufacturer of electric heaters we studied. They organized quality improvement committees, sent people to training programs, and gave speeches about the importance of being number one in quality. But quality was controlled at the plant level, and the plant managers were evaluated on volume, not on decreasing the number of heaters returned or other quality measures. Given the option to cut or slow production to deal with a quality problem, or keep production up and leave quality problems to be dealt with in the field, you can guess what plant managers chose to do. Even with all the speeches that "quality is free," and that increased quality would not lessen volume, when push came to shove, the plant managers believed what they saw and experienced, not what they heard in speeches. Quantity in the short run was what counted, not efforts to improve quality. All decisions, speeches, rewards, and plans must be consistent with the strategy before employees will understand. Managers must communicate strategy in everything they do. They must communicate it not only downward, but horizontally to other departments whose support they need, and upward to make sure the boss buys into and supports the direction they are taking.

HOW TO COMMUNICATE STRATEGY

Strategies have the power to provide a direction and to energize, but only if they are meaningful for employees. An organization's strategy must become each individual's strategy.

For employees, the strategy must be a source of pride and energy. It is the basis for each job. People must know the strategy and make decisions in their own areas concerning how to implement it. A strategy statement is a good start but it must be communicated forcefully if it is to have an impact.

Get Strategy as Psychologically Close
to the Employee as Possible

To be meaningful, strategy has to come alive in employees' jobs. The overall strategy has to be restated in terms applicable to what the employee is doing on a day-to-day basis.

A basic rule of human behavior states that the closer information is to a person, the more likely the person is to accept and use it. That means the information they collect themselves, they are most likely to believe. They are more likely to view with skepticism information they receive from their supervisor, such as performance appraisals, explanations of company policy, and progress reports, than information they collect themselves. They are least likely to accept information they receive from higher-level managers, particularly reports on the status of the organization and explanations of strategy.

Figure 3-1 presents results of research by Donald Cantor and Phillip Mirvis. They analyzed cynicism among American and European workers. They define a *cynic* as someone who believes most people will tell a lie if they can gain by doing it, that people pretend to care more about one another than they really do, and that people claim to be honest and moral but act otherwise when money is at stake. According to their research, fully 43 percent of the American work force is categorized as cynical. If this is true it is no wonder many employees do not believe what managers say. Cynics want to find out for themselves.

FIGURE 3-1 ▪ Cynicism in the Work Force*

- 43% of the overall working population fits the profile of the cynic.
- 47% of the men compared with 39% of the women are cynical.
- 60% of the minorities versus 40% of the whites are cynical.
- The less educated and lowest earners are more cynical than those in higher social economic groups.
- Young people under 24 are more cynical than baby boomers and both groups are more cynical than those age 35 or older.

---

*Donald L. Cantor and Phillip H. Mirvis, *The Cynical Americans* (San Francisco: Jossey-Bass, 1989).

For employees in general, and cynics in particular, strategy must be virtually delivered to their door steps, as close to them as possible. Top management's explanation of the strategy is a good start, but the message has to become part of each employee's job before it will be implemented. Employees must develop their own personal strategies which are consistent with the overall strategy.

Ross Perot, founder of Electronic Data Services (EDS), tells an interesting story of how he used performance requirements to communicate strategy. EDS was competing with IBM and other computer firms for a major government contract. Winning was important to EDS, as much for creating an image as for increasing business. The government had broken the contract down into seven components, each of which might be won by a different firm, or all by one firm. EDS, in turn, broke its employees into teams, assigning each team to one component. Gradually the competition was narrowed so that IBM and EDS were going head to head on each of the seven components. Perot collected his people together and gave them the performance requirement: EDS needed to win seven out of seven, or they would not accept the contract. Not five out of seven, not six out of seven, but seven out of seven. Perot explained afterwards that he wanted winning the whole contract to be each person's direct responsibility, he wanted the overall goal to be everyone's goal. By structuring the performance requirement the way he did he brought the strategy of winning one step closer to each individual. If he had accepted four or five out of seven, each team would have an out. In other words, if any team were allowed to lose, the overall goal would belong to no one. With seven out of seven as the requirement, every team knew it was their job to get the contract. The team supervisors were able to focus the efforts of their groups very effectively. EDS won seven out of seven.

Keep It Simple, Keep It Focused, Make It Memorable

The more complex a strategy is, the less people will remember and refer to it as a guide. Successful strategies are simple. Einstein set the scientific community on its head with his formula $E = MC^2$ partly because it was right, and partly because it was so simple to remember. Students could spend their time thinking about what the formula meant rather than trying to remember what it was.

The McKinsey 7'S framework (Strategy, Structure, Systems, Skills, Style, Staff, and Superordinate Goals) has become a very popular framework for analyzing organizations.[1] This framework has been the basis of several popular books. It serves as the basis for analysis in business school cases. It is used by consultants to do large-scale corporate analysis. Part of its popularity is because it is memorable. In fact, the developers consciously set developing a simple and memorable framework as one of their objectives. Strings of words are easier to memorize if they start with the same letter. Though the 7'S framework requires a little imagination and interpretation to use, it works. What is lost in logic is gained in ease of memory. The same principles apply to strategy: The elegance of a good strategy is its simplicity in use. Keep it simple, keep it focused, and make it memorable.

Use Multiple Channels to Communicate

Strategy should be woven into everything you do — speeches, presentations, interviews, discussions, meetings, rewards, plans, and so on. For example, John Buono, President of Analytical Answers, Inc. in Woburn, Massachusetts, needed multiple channels to communicate and reinforce a shift to a strategy focused on customer responsiveness. He began by reexamining the company's mission statement and revising it to reflect this new focus. Because the new mission statement was used regularly to evaluate performance, people began to view it as important. At the monthly staff meetings, time was set aside to review the new strategy. Buono set up systems to collect data on sales calls, repeat business, and new customers. At first these data were fed back every two days, but after several months the data were fed back weekly. Buono held several special events to reward and reinforce exceptional efforts toward achieving the new goals. The bonus system was revised to recognize the new strategy.

---

[1] See Robert H. Waterman, Jr., Thomas J. Peters, and Julien R. Phillips, "Structure is not Organization," *Business Horizons,* 23, no. 3 (June 1980), 14–26.

Buono used recruiting, speeches, and professional society meetings to describe the company's emphasis to new employees. In-house training sessions were developed to sharpen the focus on the customers, and the skills to understand and respond to them. Everyone having anything to do with Buono, Analytical Answers, and his people knew about the new strategy.

Use an Outside/In Strategy

If the boss tells you that you are a great worker, that carries some credibility. If one of your co-workers tells you the boss told him you're a great worker, that carries a lot more credibility. The same principle applies to strategy. Information we receive about a strategy from a third party is often more believable than information we receive directly from management. For example, George Brown, Executive Vice-President of Operations for Simpson and Williams (all fictitious names), wanted to send a message to the engineering units that he was serious about the strategies of cost control and customer responsiveness. He told them repeatedly, but did not seem to be getting the message across. It did not get through until a local newspaper interviewed Brown about what S & W was doing to meet foreign competition. Brown took the opportunity to lay out in graphic detail the competitive challenge. He explained the engineering strategy of cost control and customer responsiveness and assessed the company's progress.

Simpson and Williams was an organization that valued secrecy. No one ever talked to the press. Brown, however, did for a very specific purpose. He wanted to send a potent message to people inside the organization. In billiards or pool this would be referred to as a *ricochet shot*. Hitting the ball directly is sometimes hard or generates too much spin, causing the ball to miss its mark. Therefore, a seasoned pool player will aim the cue ball at a third ball, which then hits the target ball at the proper angle and force to sink it. Brown deliberately aimed at a third party, the press, so his message would hit the ultimate target, his engineering staff, at the most effective angle and force.

Other examples of external communication that reinforce internal strategy are Xerox's "Team Xerox," Ford's "Quality is Job 1," and 3M's ads on innovation. Not only do these ads convey a message to the public, they send a powerful message to employees about what is important in the organization.

COMMUNICATE HORIZONTALLY

When we talk about communicating the strategy most people think about vertical communication. We would be remiss to leave it at that; an equally strong need exists to communicate horizontally between departments or groups who are dependent on each other. You need the active support of others to accomplish your strategy. They need to understand what you are trying to accomplish and where they fit. You also need to understand where you fit into their work. For example, one general manager we worked with in a parts manufacturing company had a practice of meeting regularly one on one with the heads of his functional organization but spent little time meeting with all of the functional area heads together. The functional area heads naturally focused on their own activities. Even though they tried to coordinate with other units, they were too busy with their own concerns to worry about anyone else. Major problems resulted. Manufacturing planned to move out of an underutilized space; at the same time the engineering organization planned to improve the efficiency of the machinery and layout of equipment in the very same space. The marketing organization reoriented advertising, placing emphasis on certain accessories. This was not communicated to manufacturing in time for them to change production schedules, notify suppliers, and manufacture the needed accessories. As a result, the first several thousand units had to be shipped without the required accessories.

Numerous operating problems resulted from a lack of horizontal communication, but the most serious was the antagonism between the departments. Each felt the other departments were not supportive. Even when they met to iron out their differences, the meetings degenerated into finger pointing.

The general manager can be faulted for choosing to operate one on one, and not taking the time to force communication between functions. On the other hand, it is impossible for one person to serve as the link between functional groups that are heavily interdependent on each other, particularly if that one person is the boss. Functional heads have to accept some responsibility. Every time a problem between units was raised, the tendency was to bounce it up to the boss. People jockeyed for positions and wasted valuable time politically maneuvering, rather than sitting down with their counterparts in other functions and solving problems. In spite of the tremendous need for managers to talk with each other across functions, formal management practices emphasize vertical communication. Management by objectives is most often an up-and-down process between boss and subordinates, rather than a horizontal sharing of objectives. The catch-all phrase "bottoms-up communication" also reinforces the hierarchical process. It refers to subordinates talking to bosses within organization lines and places little emphasis on subordinates from different functional areas talking to each other.

Even strategic planning frameworks tend to concentrate either within functional areas or for the business as a whole. Marketing strategy, manufacturing strategy, and technology strategy are often interpreted to mean how each of these functions can optimize its contributions to the corporate strategy. But the functions are interdependent, they must support each other. The question is not how they can optimize their strategy, but how together they can optimize the corporate strategy.

We do not mean to create the impression that no one is concerned about cross-functional communication. Techniques such as team building and horizontal task forces often help horizontal communication. But they tend to be used as ad hoc, temporary methods only incidentally related to strategic issues. Yet, it is around strategic issues that organizations must communicate cross-functionally.

The press of schedule and the need for help, parts, or resources can force functional groups to communicate, but their communication focuses on the short term and as soon as the pressure stops, the communication stops. No pressure exists for checking strategic assumptions and maintaining horizontal communications. In a division of a manufacturing company we worked with, people from the nine functional areas noted in Figure 3-2 were asked to rate the information flow between their area and the other eight functional areas. They rated the information flow on operational communication (communication about how the work was being done) and on strategic communication (communication on what the objectives and strategies were). The scores are noted in Figure 3-2.

Note that in all but the one case in Manufacturing, operational horizontal communication is rated better than strategic horizontal communication and nothing is rated very highly. Each department did not have adequate information about what other departments were doing. Without an understanding of what other units are trying to accomplish, departments cannot support each other.

FIGURE 3-2 ▪ Amount of Information Available
from Other Departments

	Operational	Strategic
Quality	3.6	2.5
MIS	3.3	2.2
Engineering	3.2	2.4
Manufacturing	3.0	3.0
Finance	2.8	2.2
Sales	2.8	2.7
Materials	2.6	2.0
Personnel	2.5	2.3
Public Relations	1.5	1.2

Rating   1. Grossly inadequate
           2. Inadequate
           3. Adequate
           4. Very satisfactory
           5. Too much

Source of data: Used by permission from Strategic Communication Survey (Frohman Associates, Lexington, MA).

Get Agreement on the Words

Communication across functional boundaries has the same problems as communication between people of different cultures. People in different functions come from different cultures and speak different languages. The first challenge is getting everyone to understand the language.

The president of a pharmaceutical company we worked with decided to tackle this problem head on. He wanted to make sure everyone could talk with each other. They spent the first day of a three-day strategic planning session defining terms like: *plan, accountability, responsibility, coordination, acceptable,* and so on. When they started early Monday morning, they thought it would only take a couple of hours. As they labored long into the night, it was painfully apparent how little understanding and agreement existed about basic management vocabulary.

Part of the value of sitting down together to hammer out definitions is clarifying confusion over the meaning of words. The expression "the problem is one of semantics" is frequently descriptive of the heart of misunderstandings about strategy.

The first step is to have a common vocabulary. When someone talks about *strengths,* there needs to be agreement on what the definition of *strengths* is and what the word itself means. The terms *customers, distinctive competence, objective, strategy, plans,* and *markets* need to be defined. To the president without a technical background *R&D* may mean servicing customers' needs. On the other hand, to the manager of the R&D organization, R&D may be something closer to applied research. It is the imprecision of these abstract business terms which makes effective linkage between the strategies of different parts of the organization very difficult. Consequently, the first order of business in communicating cross-functionally is agreement on terms and their definitions. A glossary of key terms is an essential part of any strategy discussion.

We recommend that any time people from different units get together, start with a review of vocabulary. Only after terminology and assumptions have been written down and agreed upon can substantive strategy formulation begin.

Use Cross-Functional Teams Effectively

To get effective, strategic communication across functions, mechanisms that draw people together on a regular basis are needed. Monthly or quarterly meetings are not enough. Many companies are using teams with representatives from a variety of functional areas to facilitate better horizontal communications. For example, to develop a new product, a team is often put together from the following functions: engineering, manufacturing, materials management, finance, quality control, service, and perhaps even an outside supplier.

Many companies use cross-functional teams very effectively for a wide range of purposes such as cutting costs, bringing out new products, and improving quality. Honeywell uses "Tiger Teams," and Boeing's version of cross-functional teams are called "Skunk Works." The Big Three auto makers use PDTs (product development teams) to coordinate the development for a new vehicle. Rather than Marketing handing off a new product idea to Engineering, and Engineering then developing a set of designs which is passed on to Manufacturing, and so on down the line, a team consisting of representatives from all the departments works together simultaneously to design, engineer, manufacture, and market a product. Instead of functioning in sequence and often in isolation from each other, from the start, the cross-functional team works together to design, manufacture, and market a product.

Team members work around a common set of goals and schedules. The team itself, rather than the organizational hierarchy, focuses and coordinates the efforts of its members. The traditional vertical flow of communication and decisions from the top down is complemented with an extensive horizontal exchange of communication and decisions across the functional boundaries within the team. You can tell how serious an organization is about cross-functional coordination by the power they give to these teams.

Some organizations have heavyweight teams. They have the power to allocate budget, control, schedule, and make decisions. They are held accountable for project results. Peoples' careers rise and fall based on the success of the group.

Some organizations have middleweight teams. They make and are responsible for implementing decisions, but must get approval for budget expenditures. People are assigned to the team, but know their career progression is determined by their functional boss, not the success of the team. Consequently, they are always checking back in to make sure they are representing the function properly.

Many organizations have lightweight teams. Members are solely representatives of their function. They must check everything with their functional boss. They have no power to make decisions; they act solely as spokespersons for their functional perspective. Lightweight teams do not help cross-functional communication much. They identify areas of disagreement but have no power to resolve them.

Just bringing a group together and giving them an assignment does not result in effective teamwork. They have to be given the responsibility and resources to succeed and the opportunity to fail; obviously heavyweight teams are going to be made more effective than lightweight teams. Here are suggestions we have found to improve the success of cross-functional teams.

1. Include an individual's work in teams as part of each one's performance evaluation. People should be evaluated on the basis of their work in teams in addition to performance in their regular jobs. They

should be assessed on their contribution to the project and on their ability to work as team players. Individuals whose own performance is at the expense of the team should receive poor performance ratings.

2. **Reward a team as a single unit.** When team members are rewarded together, the message is clear that the team's performance is the responsibility of all of its members. In this way, *each* member of the team is on the line. The whole team, not just the leader, is responsible for results. At Arrowstreet, a Massachusetts firm of architects and planners, a bonus pool is created for each project. The size of the bonus pool depends on the overall success of the project. Within certain broad guidelines the project manager has the discretion to divide up the pool depending on the contribution of each individual team member to the project.

3. **Give team members the authority to speak for their department.** If members simply represent their department and have to get the approval of their boss for each decision, the team may never form a cohesive unit. They have to be able to make decisions and drive them to implementation. "I have had an opportunity to watch a number of teams very closely," says George Fernald, a retired Senior Vice President from Polaroid, "and the difference in effectiveness is like night and day when the members of a team—regardless of their rank—are able to speak for their department."

4. **Give teams an integral place in the organization's structure which appropriately recognizes their responsibility.** Organization charts at aerospace firms like Boeing and Lockheed reflect the responsibilities which are assigned to teams to manufacture and assemble specific sections of an aircraft.

5. **Share with team members all relevant information that will affect their decisions.** We have found that some managers at the top are reluctant to share the specifics of their strategy and business plans for fear this information will be "leaked" to the competition. This failure to provide teams with the full picture sometimes means that a team's decisions have to be reversed. At a computer company where a team selected a supplier of a new series of parts, failure to share the fact that strategy was shifting to greater reliance on internal manufacturing resulted in a reversal of the team's decision. Although the team members understood the reasons for management's change in policy, once it was explained to them, they were upset at not having had access to this information when they needed it.

6. **Focus training programs on networking, conflict management, and project-coordination skills vital for effective cross-functional team management.** Companies ranging from Apple and Atari to Colgate-Palmolive and International Paper use training programs in skills needed for effective teamwork.

Using these suggestions will result in some unexpected benefits. Cross-functional teams are an effective tool for developing future managers. Most people moving up through the ranks follow the specialist route, so participation on a team represents an opportunity to gain a broader perspective and to develop a clearer understanding of the issues facing a corporation. The team experience also provides people with the opportunity to gain valuable managerial skills which will be helpful in future assignments.

Rotate People Across Functional Departments

Rotating people across functional departments provides an excellent opportunity for them to establish informal communication networks throughout the organization. Exposure to other functions helps them to know who to contact when help or information is needed.

Rotation programs often meet with resistance. To be successful they need the sponsorship of top management. Rotation must be seen as their program. This requires the involvement of top management in selecting participants from highly rated people and regular meetings with a top manager to help them continue learning from their jobs.

Include Cross-Functional Peer Evaluation
in Performance Reviews

Evaluation of performance has historically encompassed only specific unit-focused goals. The opinions from those in other units have been neglected. It is essential for people to know that they are expected to communicate and coordinate laterally. One good way of getting the message across is to have peers outside a person's department evaluate his or her contributions to their work. Talk about the importance of cross-functional communication is good, but people will not really believe it until it starts counting in promotional opportunities, compensation, and status.

Take an Accountant to Lunch

The Operations Department of a major large equipment manufacturing company was having severe trouble with the corporate and division Finance Departments. Finance just did not seem to understand the capital-investment needs, pricing policies, and budgeting requirements of Operations. They just could not work with people from Finance. Three of the mid-level managers attended a mid-level management program where they were asked to identify their most critical problems and develop suggested solutions. They quickly identified Finance as their problem and could identify no solutions. Another manager offhandedly said that it sounded like what they needed to do was take an accountant to lunch.

Why? To find out how they thought and what pressures they were under. By understanding them they could better work together.

Operations adopted the program. The people in Finance were, of course, suspicious at first, but Operations did it right. They did not try to sell or convince; their purpose at lunch was to understand Finance and how it fit into the business. The payoff? Operations gradually learned how Finance made decisions and what pressures they were under. They learned how to work with Finance. Some of the Operations managers even found out Finance people were "not so bad after all."

We do not mean to suggest Finance is the root of all problems and you should concentrate on establishing relationships with them. Take an engineer to lunch, take a marketer to lunch, a supplier, a lawyer, and so on. Make it common business practice to get to know those on whom you depend. Remember the purpose of the lunch is not to convince them to support you, or to sell your ideas. It is simply to understand how they do their work and what pressures they face. You might even be bold enough to ask them how you could help them get their job done. You will be surprised at how attentive people get when the question is, "How can I help you?"

COMMUNICATING UPWARD

One person who so obviously needs to buy into your strategy that we hesitate even mentioning him or her is your boss. Sad to say, however, we find many managers working hard to implement their strategy, assuming the boss knows what they are trying to accomplish. Do not make assumptions, it is better to check. You have nothing to lose and everything to gain. If you have any reservations at all (such as, I will look foolish; of course the boss already knows; I do not have time; and so on), think how you would respond if some of your subordinates came to you. They are not clear on what is to be accomplished. They present their understanding and ask if that is correct. Of course you would take time to clarify and get them on the right path. You would probably also think well of them for asking and not wasting their time going down the wrong paths. Your boss wants to hear from you as well. Always keep the boss informed.

IS THE MESSAGE GETTING ACROSS?

The most threatened part of communicating a strategy is evaluation, asking the question: "Is the message getting across?" Threats are inherent in evaluations because in each evaluation lies the possible revelation that someone has not performed. Many managers are tempted to assume people understand strategy. It is easier to pretend everything is fine and continue working, rather than taking time to find out.

However, ample evidence exists showing that the further down in the organization a message travels, the less the message gets across. The data from a high-technology firm presented in Figures 3–3A and 3–3B illustrate this point. Based on these data, it should not be surprising that the lower levels of the organization were not actively trying to implement the strategy.

Evaluation mechanisms should be established whenever you plan communication. Without an evaluation, the sender does not know if people understand and are committed to the strategy. Following are four guidelines which will make evaluation useful to the sender of communication:

1. Evaluate the receiver's understanding of and commitment to the strategy. Evaluating both of these provides information on how meaningful the strategy is to employees.

2. Relate the evaluation directly to the strategy. One very good way to communicate strategy is to state it in an evaluation question. For example, rather than asking if the receiver knows what the strategy is, explain "Our unit's strategy is 23 percent market share with a quality index of 97 percent. Are you aware of this?" Obviously stating

FIGURE 3–3A ▪ Understanding Strategy

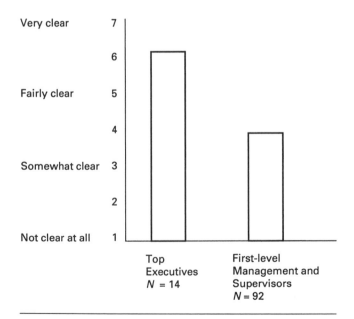

Question: Is the strategy of the organization clear to you?

Very clear	7	
	6	
Fairly clear	5	
	4	
Somewhat clear	3	
	2	
Not clear at all	1	

Top
Executives
N = 14

First-level
Management and
Supervisors
N = 92

Source of data: Used by permission from *Strategy Action Questionnaire* (Frohman Associates, Lexington, MA).

FIGURE 3–3B ▪ Understanding Strategy

Question: Do you feel well informed about the strategy of the organization?

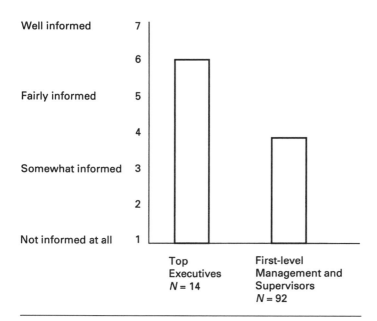

Top Executives *N* = 14	First-level Management and Supervisors *N* = 92

Source of data: Used by permission from *Strategy Action Questionnaire* (Frohman Associates, Lexington, MA).

the question this way will cause people to give more positive answers. Many people who construct questionnaires would find fault with this approach; however, we find that what you are doing is communicating the strategy. What you lose in accuracy, you more than make up in increased understanding on the part of the survey participants. Remember that you communicate by the questions you ask.

3. Involve the employees in interpreting the data. Make them responsible for changes that will improve communications. Encourage managers to use the evaluation data to open discussions and get people involved to raise the level of understanding.

4. Focus on what you can do to help others understand the strategy.

Following these guidelines will help you translate evaluation into positive results. For example, the reactions to the data presented in Figures 3–3A and 3–3B could be: "Those dummies, I did my job, I developed a clear strategy and spent time communicating; too bad I have such unmotivated, unskilled workers." That reaction of course will accomplish very little.

Rather than stepping back and figuring out how better to handle the situation, a manager reacting this way will probably tend to continue doing what he or she is already doing, only with more effort. This is similar to the reaction some people have when they are not understood by a person who doesn't speak their language. Instead of changing the phrase or attempting a few foreign words, they repeat what they already said but only this time louder.

Another reaction is more likely to lead to positive results. Ask yourself: "What do I need to change in order to help them understand the message?" If they do not understand what you are saying, rephrase it, repeat it, but use different terminology, different examples, and different emotions. Do not just say the same thing louder. Do something different. If the old way of delivering the message is not working, find a new way.

Asking what you need to change is important for the simple reason that you can control your behavior much more easily than you can control theirs. Waiting for them to change may be a very long wait.

THE PAYOFF

A clearly communicated strategy has many payoffs. Carefully communicating and monitoring to make sure the message gets across is worth the effort. If people know where they are going they can manage themselves to get there. They have a sense of direction and purpose. If they do not know where they are going they can only respond to controls. Budgets provide many examples of the advantage of having people respond to a strategy, rather than responding to controls. A budget only tells you how much the organization thinks should be spent; it does not tell you where the organization is going and how it will get there. Comparing actions against a budget, rather than a strategy, can only indicate how much money has been spent or whether more is available. It does not tell you whether you are getting where you want to go. It does not tell you where to cut, how to shift resources, or whether increased expenditures are needed. It is management consistent with the perspective of control, not empowerment.

A Sense of Direction

The difference between complying with controls and understanding the strategy becomes very obvious when employees run into situations where conforming to the rules is problematic, or when two or more rules require conflicting actions. For example, many organizations have rules about cost, quality, and customer service; that is, keep costs down, keep quality up, and keep the customer happy. Budgets, procedures, and systems are set up to control, monitor, and support each of these objectives. Everything works fine until keeping the customer happy or providing quality costs more than is in the budget. Then compliance with one objective requires violation of another. If the manager has no strategy by which to prioritize objectives, the budget will usually wind up at the top of the list. Budget wins because it can be counted, is visible, and is understood by most managers.

We have all seen examples of people making trade-off decisions guided by an overall strategy. The airline stewardess gives a free drink to a passenger who has been particularly helpful with a mother and three children sitting next to him, though rules say no free drinks. A cashier accepts a return of merchandise bought on sale by a regular customer, even though the policy for the sale was no returns. An engineer completes a crucial project and his manager tells him to take the weekend off, take his wife out to eat at a good restaurant, go to a play, and submit the bills on an expense report. The rules say no nonbusiness expenses will be approved.

The airline has an overriding strategy of customer service, the store a strategy of maintaining long-term relationships with customers, and the manufacturing firm a dominant strategy of recognizing and rewarding performance. Strategies give managers a sense of direction that help them make difficult choices and guide their behavior in tough situations.

Sense of Importance

A second benefit of a clearly communicated strategy is the sense of importance it creates. People are motivated when they see themselves as part of an overall purpose, something bigger than what they can individually accomplish. An old story best illustrates the power a sense of purpose can create.

During World War II, a colonel walking through an airplane factory stopped to ask workers, all doing the same thing, what their job was and he received three different responses:

- "Putting screws in the wing."
- "Making the world's best plane."
- "Helping win the war."

Imagine the difference in motivation, involvement, and performance of workers who believed their job was to put screws in the wing and those who saw it as winning the war. A good strategy gives a sense of importance by providing employees a framework within which to do their job. This framework transcends the day-to-day activities and gives meaning and purpose to the work.

The Anchor Hocking Corporation had a strategy of good customer and supplier relations. That strategy was brought to life by a van driver we met. His main job was to pick visitors up at the airport and drive them to the corporate headquarters. The company bought a new van every three years. The driver kept the van spotless and perfectly maintained. He washed it, changed the oil every 2,000 miles, and made repairs whenever needed. The driver was the first contact customers and suppliers coming to corporate headquarters had with the Anchor Hocking Corporation, and he went the extra mile to make sure they started with a good impression. He used a citizen band radio in the van to communicate with corporate headquarters informing them of the arrival and safe departure of visitors. He also used it to call ahead to make arrangements for flights, pick ups, baggage handling, or any other coordination needed. We never learned his real name, but his call name on the radio was certainly appropriate—"Anchor Man." He felt he was one of Anchor Hocking's most important employees because he introduced visitors to the company. He went out of his way to make a good impression, leaving no detail unattended. As a result, visitors to Anchor Hocking left feeling positive about both "Anchor Man" and the company.

Focus of Energy

The third payoff from a clearly communicated strategy is focused energy. The magic of management is getting people to pull together in a common direction. There is much truth to the 80/20 rule formulated by the economist Pareto: 80 percent of the productive work will be done by 20 percent of the people; 80 percent of the business payoff will come from 20 percent of the products; 80 percent of what an individual accomplishes will be accomplished in 20 percent of his or her work time. A clearly communicated strategy can shift the balance in these percentages: well-directed, focused people will devote more of their time to crucial activities, organizations will be more efficient, and performance will improve.

The principle of using strategy to focus energy and increase performance applies to small groups as well as large organizations. If people have a common understanding of what they are trying to accomplish, they will find it much easier to work together. For example, Figure 3–4 presents an analysis of 32 product development teams (PDTs) in a large industrial firm. Product development teams are composed of individuals from different functions and units within an organization brought together to develop a new product or component. As can be seen, teams with the highest performance rating (they keep to a schedule, successfully reduce costs, meet organizational objectives), functioned well as a group, and better understood their own strategy and purpose. They had a clear focus.

The differences in understanding and clarity of the PDTs' goals and strategy are evident in the following quotes, the first from the member of a PDT with a high performance rating and the second from the member of a poorer performing team.

> Understanding the concepts and goals has awakened business sense in people who had no vision of where we were going before. We are better able to work toward a common goal. (Member of a better performing team.)

FIGURE 3-4 ▪ Clarity of Goals and Strategy in High- and Low-
Performing Product Development Teams
(*N* = Number of Teams)

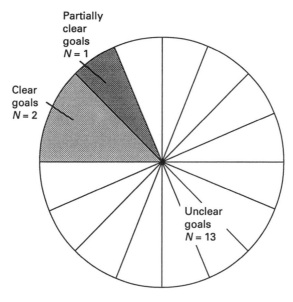

Low Performing Teams

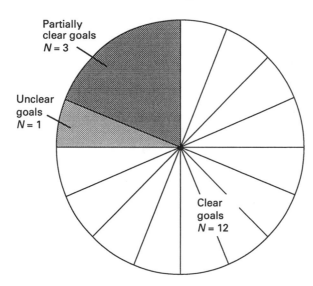

High Performing Teams

Source of data: Interviews with team members, Frohman Associates, Lexington, MA.

The focus and priorities for each member are different. We do not know what the right goals are. (Member of a poorer performing team.)

Many people are in the thick of very thin things. They are straightening deck chairs on the Titanic as it sinks below the surface. A well-communicated strategy has the ability to get them into the thick of very important things.

Manager's Checklist

1. Identify an important strategic message you would like to communicate. Get a group together and brainstorm to identify as many channels as possible to communicate the message. Be creative. People remember actions that deviate from the norm, so use methods and modes never used before.

2. Next time you speak with an employee group, ask them what they are doing to help implement the strategy. For example, if the strategy is customer service, ask them what they are doing or can do to deliver value to the ultimate customer. To make a two-way discussion, share with them what you are doing. Be specific; give them concrete examples, not explanations of corporate policies and procedures. Tell them what you as an individual are doing.

3. Make sure those supplying your resources, information, and products understand what you are trying to accomplish. Make sure you understand what those whom you supply are trying to accomplish.

4. Form a cross-functional team to deal with a real problem and give the team power to make decisions and drive implementation. If you already have cross-functional teams in place, carefully analyze whether they are lightweight, middleweight, or heavyweight teams. Make them heavyweight teams.

5. Write your strategy on the top half of a piece of paper. On the bottom half write what you plan to do to implement the strategy. Give the sheet to your boss and ask for comments.

6. Commit yourself to rotating some of your best people to other units and functions. Two approaches can be taken to moving people. First, put people in the job who already have the skills and potential ability to perform well. Second, put people in the jobs whom you want to grow; give them a challenge and help them learn. Most of the time you will undoubtedly take the first approach, but for some of your key people take the second. Identify jobs that will help them stretch and at

the same time improve cross-functional communication and coordination. Take a risk. The payoff to the organization and the individual will be high.

7. Commit yourself to evaluating your communication. Establish mechanisms for evaluating your communication success. Evaluate both understanding and commitment to the message. Involving others in helping you evaluate their performance will increase their own commitment to making sure the message gets across.

CHAPTER 4

Key #2: Leverage Key Performers

*H*elping people to reach high performance is best done by getting out front, reaching back, giving people general guidance, and then helping them come to where you are. This is the pull approach to leadership. Pulling people to results requires far different help from others than pushing. Pushing requires tight controls, rewards, and tremendous force. It's like trying to move a herd of sheep from the back. In order to get the sheep where you want them to be, you need a team of very competent sheep dogs, yelping at the heels of the sheep to keep them in line. You need strong horses that can turn and dodge, and skilled riders to control them. The problem, of course, is the sheep have no idea where they are going. They can only discover the path by trying one and seeing if you turn them back. Your ability to control is limited by how fast the dogs and horses can run. The only way to move the sheep faster or change their direction is by increasing control, getting more dogs and faster horses. As soon as the dogs and horses stop, the sheep stop.

Pulling, instead of pushing, puts you in front. In order to implement strategy and get results, you only need to get employees to come where you are. You lead by communicating. They can see you and know where they have to go. They can select the best path to get there. Your focus need not be on tight controls. What you need is a general direction, clearly communicated to key people in the right positions that can help guide others.

This is referred to as the parade theory of leadership: Managers need to get in front of the parade. Sometimes, the parade only needs someone to help them coordinate their steps; they know where they are going and what they have to do. Other times the parade needs someone out front to show them where to go and teach them what they should do. Sometimes no parade exists. Managers have to create it and then get in front. In any case, a manager's position is out front, guiding and leading—not in back pushing.

Next, get your best people in the key positions which give them the most leverage. Get them to help you pull and the rest will be drawn to the strategy, managing themselves along the way. They will not waste time and resources veering down the wrong paths only to discover later that they are not where they are supposed to be. You will not need extensive controls and elaborately contrived reward systems. Once people in key positions catch the vision, they will draw others in and the movement will cascade throughout the organization. Having your best people in key positions is the critical factor for pulling strategy to results.

IDENTIFY KEY POSITIONS

Key positions are those on which the success or failure of the strategy is built. Of course, people in every position can make important contributions but a few are in leveraged positions that determine the success of the whole organization. What people in these positions do affects what many others do. The first step in successful strategy implementation is to identify these positions. They will vary depending on what strategy is adopted.

The financial services industry provides many examples of how strategy determines key positions. In the 1970s, most insurance companies began automating and changing their management systems to increase efficiency. Prior to automation, agents sold life insurance policies and secretarial and clerical employees completed the documentation and handled claims. The strategy was to maximize sales and minimize the cost of processing transactions; hence, the key management positions were in sales, managing and motivating agents, and processing, making the vast secretarial pool who did the processing as efficient as possible. With automation, the key positions shifted. The agents selling life insurance were still important but now sophisticated computer systems and processing capability were needed. Managers who could lead and efficiently run information processing groups became absolutely essential to the organization's survival.

In the 1980s, deregulation created the need for a second major shift. Many insurance companies changed their strategies (and often their names) to become "full-service financial institutions." The insurance agent became a financial advisor. Now key positions entailed the responsibility for coordinating multiple services, from investment bankers to real estate brokers and medical coverage specialists, so the organization could deliver full service.

In the 1990s competition is projected to become even more intense, as international firms with their tremendous financial reserves enter the

American market. Strategists with the ability to sense the environment and respond to it are needed. To truly and successfully respond to increased competition from a global perspective, positions focusing on the external environment will become critical. Some areas of operation will grow, while others will shrink. Simply announcing the company is a global institution and that it will be internationally competitive is not enough.

Following are examples of how varying strategies in different industries determine key positions.[1] In the mining of precious ores, prospecting is crucial. The most efficient processing capabilities will be useless without the silver or gold-laden ore. In the steel industry, ore is easily found and readily available. The key positions are in processing: Turning ore into steel. Some Japanese firms have become masters in processing. They buy ore from the United States, ship it to Japan, process it, ship it back, and sell it to us cheaper than we can do it ourselves.

In the soft-drink industry, the key positions are in distribution. If people in those positions do not perform, the whole organization fails. The motto of firms in the soft-drink industry is "within an arm's length of desire." They want to get the soft drink as close to consumers as possible, knowing that consumers are likely to drink whatever is most readily available. They exert a major effort developing relationships with fast-food establishments, invest millions in dispensing machines, and develop elaborate computer programs to manage the flow of their product.

The soft-drink and fast-food industries provide a good example of the importance of having competent people in key positions, in these cases the distribution function. Someone came up with a way to get drinks even closer to the customer, decreasing cost and increasing customer satisfaction simultaneously. They let the customer fill the glasses. The profit margin and the distribution efficiency goes up by selling customers the cup and moving the dispensing machine into the customer area. They are substantially reducing their costs by reducing the cost of labor and at the same time getting the product even closer to the customer. Customer satisfaction goes up because they gain control over the amount of ice, they can mix different types of drinks, and the cost of refills has gone down.

In the cosmetics industry the motto is "In the factory we produce perfume, and in the store we sell hope." They are selling an image. It is no wonder that firms in the cosmetics industry have large advertising budgets. They have to create the image. If you are in cosmetics and do not have top performers in advertising and marketing, your chances for success are minimal.

Depending on your strategy, research, processing, distribution, or marketing may contain the key leverage positions. If these jobs are per-

---

[1]See Stan Davis, *Future Perfect* (Reading, MA: Addison-Wesley, 1989) for a full discussion of value added as the basis of distinctive competence.

formed well, everything else follows. If these are performed poorly, the whole organization fails.

Identifying key positions requires an understanding of the buyers of your product or service. Why do they buy the product or service? Consumers may have a number of different reasons. They may like the product's characteristics, they may be attracted by the reliability and quality of the product, or perhaps they are willing to pay for the convenience and availability of the product, or they simply like the image owning the product gives them. The key is understanding the customers. What do they want and what are they willing to pay for? That is a simple concept often forgotten by people who make products or deliver services. In reality your customers do not want your product or service for its own sake. They have problems to solve and opportunities to take advantage of and are looking for products and services that can help them. If, in their search, they decide yours comes closest to solving their problems, they will choose yours.

Let Customers Identify Key Positions

To identify key positions you will have to be very clear about exactly what and why the customer is purchasing your product or service. For example, words such as *quality, reliability, state of the art, services,* and *convenience* are useful starting points, but more precise definitions are needed. Where appearance is a factor, quality may mean how the product looks, how cleanly the features are appointed. Where service life is important, quality may mean how durable the product is and how long it can be used before it needs to be repaired. Where the absence of contamination is important, quality could mean a very high level of purity—for example, packaged food. Hence, it is vital that you very clearly understand your market and your customers' purchasing decisions.

Key positions will be those which add the most value to the customer. Go back for a minute to our mining example. Let us assume, to illustrate the concept of value from the customer's perspective, that you are in the mining business but unfortunately you do not have people who are good at finding gold. However, you *have* built a skill base in the processing of gold. You can process dirt and rocks and smelt gold bars better and cheaper than anyone else.

You decide to open a processing plant and sign contracts with local gold miners. They are better than you at finding gold so let them do that and you will specialize in processing. As you visit the miners you discover one critical question they keep asking: Who will pay the transportation charge?

Why is that such a critical question? Because moving all the dirt and rocks to your processing plant costs money and it is an expense that adds absolutely no value for the customer. They could care less where the gold is processed. The price of gold is fixed. Gold is a commodity. All gold bars are the same. The transportation costs come right out of profits and be-cause there is very little gold in a ton of earth, the transportation cost will be high.

The same is true for advertising. No amount of advertising will con-vince buyers to pay more for your gold. Having an advertising department is a waste of money. Your key positions are in exploration.

The risk companies run in not carefully identifying their key positions necessary for successful implementation of the strategy is that when cost pressures increase, they will allow performance in key positions to erode. For example, a West Coast company producing bits used to drill for oil, in an effort to cut personnel, offered early retirement incentives to many of their senior engineers. Through many years of experience, these senior engineers had the knowledge of what worked and what didn't in the con-struction of oil drill bits. Their work was more art than science. It took many years of working on the design boards for engineers to understand what would make an oil drill bit fail.

The key criteria customers consider when buying oil drill bits are their reliability and dependability. They are used hundreds and thousands of feet below the surface drilling for oil. Each time the bit broke, the work would come to a halt as it was brought to the surface and replaced. With-out fully appreciating that senior engineers provided the mature judgment and technological perspective that kept the organization in business, top management of the company provided incentives for the vast majority of them to leave. In only two years, the organization was in serious trouble. Performance of its bits started to deteriorate. Examining what was going wrong, they realized the engineering talent that had provided critical judg-ment had left the company. The company wound up hiring back some of the engineers it had paid a premium to retire early.

MOVE TOP PERFORMERS
INTO KEY POSITIONS

Once key positions are identified, there is no magic involved in getting top performers into them; you can move them, develop them, or buy them. The quickest way is to identify top performers and move them into key positions. We have heard many reactions to this simple proposal. Most common is "How do I know who my top performers are?" It is not our purpose to detail the many ways of evaluating performance. If you need help in this area, we would refer you to *The Performance Management Source-book*.[2] These sources will be helpful, but our experience has been that most

---

[2] Craig E. Schneier, Richard W. Beatty, and Lloyd S. Baird, *The Performance Management Sourcebook* (Amherst, MA: Human Resource Development Press, 1987).

managers know who their best performers are—they are the ones who are producing. If you do not know, get some help.

Others who have trouble with this simple approach usually say things like: Easier said than done; I cannot move people across functional boundaries; all my good people are too junior; we cannot skip levels; my top performers are on the wrong track; we would really mess up the career paths around here if we moved them.

Nonsense, you are doing more harm than good when your best people are not in your key positions. Recently, GMFanuc Robotics identified sales and marketing as their critical challenges. They had good products but were losing market share because of their lack of marketing ability. They needed someone who understood the business and could rejuvenate the sales force. They found several managers who knew the product, worked well with customers, and could lead the marketing effort. They did not let the fact that one was from accounting, another from R&D, and another from operations stop them from moving them into sales jobs.

When trying to fill a key position, think about the best person for the job. Forget about organization protocol. Move people up multiple levels in one promotion if they are the best person for a key job. This creates a constructive sense that performance counts. To support this emphasis on performance, base bonus eligibility on potential to contribute to the success of the business, not seniority or rank.

Another option is to have people take on multiple assignments if they cannot be moved. Kevin Ostby, who successfully spearheaded part of the U.S. automotive sales for GMFanuc, was needed in Europe to help support the aggressive sales force there. Because of family considerations, he could not move immediately. So, he was assigned there on a part-time basis. He spent one week a month helping the sales effort in Europe. While it was personally demanding for Kevin, he got the experience and GMFanuc got the best performer to fill a key position when it was needed.

The message is clear: Move your top performers into key jobs. Do not let tradition, personal ties, organization structure, or inertia stand in the way. Sometimes the moves must be made very delicately, but they must be made. In one organization we are familiar with, the head of a business unit critical to the organization was not performing well. He was a scientist who did not enjoy nor execute well the administrative responsibilities of managing a whole business unit. The head of research and development for the business unit was the obvious replacement. The problem was what to do with the boss. The solution was that after three very delicate discussions, the two switched jobs. Both are performing better. While this is a rare occurrence, it can be done.

One caution: As you move people, make sure you are doing it based on their ability to perform in the new capacity and not based on their ability to do the jobs they are in.

There Is No One Person for All Seasons

There are many examples of managers who have tried to make the transition from one industry to another but who have failed. One reason is the different orientations required by managers facing different business conditions. For example, we know a hard-hitting entrepreneurial type who has been very successful managing the fast growth of his unit. The company faced major challenges in their more mature core businesses. The market was declining. The business challenge was to consolidate multiple units, drive efficiency, continue to service the present client base, but move them to the new products. Based on his past success, our entrepreneur was given the job. He failed miserably. Rather than cut expenses and consolidate, he continued to invest in new equipment. The unit continued its very aggressive marketing campaign. It was as if he did not believe management and he was going to prove them wrong. He set out to prove that the unit was not dying and could be turned around. Of course, what he was doing was cannibalizing sales from the new products. He was building an empire to support a product the organization intended to withdraw from the market.

When positioning people to help you implement strategy, you must be very clear about what they can do well. Do not base your decision on how well they implemented other strategies. Base it on how well you think they can help you implement your current strategy. For example, Chase Manhattan brought in a man with entrepreneurial skills when they decided to reorient their retail banking business from a low-margin operation, in which the emphasis was on keeping costs down, to a much more expansion-oriented business. Corning Glass, when seeking a manager to head its optical fibers business, selected a manager who showed entrepreneurial flair to head a business that needed to be aggressively built. Texas Instruments is reported to use the product life-cycle curve to assign managers to new jobs. As the product moves through different phases of its life cycle—from inception through rapid growth, to slower growth, to maturity—managers with different orientations are necessary to get the most out of the business. Texas Instruments learned this lesson the hard way when it placed a manager who was oriented toward research and innovation in charge of a business that required tight controls. As a result, the company was investing money at a time when what was required was carefully watching the costs and getting the value from the investments already made in the product.

Another example is Data Resources Group, a part of International Paper. DRG grew from a small entrepreneurial company to a business needing controls and cost efficiencies. The entrepreneur who headed that part of the business was busy pursuing innovative ideas around the world, instead of spending time disciplining the organization, dealing with new competitive threats, and building the talent of subordinates. The situation deteriorated to a point that the president to whom he reported moved him into a position where his creativity and innovative talents could be better utilized. A manager better able to focus on profit and efficiency was brought in.

DEVELOP TOP PERFORMERS

Another option is to develop top performers. Steve Jacks (fictitious name), for example, manages a multibillion dollar company in Canada. He sells consumer products in an increasingly competitive market. The Japanese and others are undercutting his prices with comparable products. In response, Jacks has devised a strategy which will win back his competitive position. The battle plan is ready. His problem is that he does not have enough top performers to fill key positions. In Jacks's own words, "We do not have the hard chargers to carry it out."

Jacks has several examples. He could not find enough experienced managers to put together a joint venture which had major business potential. Good new products were delayed because he could find no one who knew how to move them into production. He could not identify managers who were ready to fill key positions opened by recent retirements. Jacks and his staff were disappointed and worried about the organization's future.

Jacks asked us and a third consultant, Mark Frohman, to take a hard-headed look at the situation. Were the number of hard chargers limited? If so, why? If not, who were they? And, most importantly, what could be done to solve the problem for both the short term and the long term?

We poured over hundreds of pages of data. We sorted through hiring, firing, training, promotion, and career figures. We interviewed staff at all levels from all functions. What we found surprised Jacks and his staff. The company hired top talent and placed them in appropriate jobs. They provided training and rewards for new skills. They spent money making sure they understood the customer and the competitive challenge. Everything seemed to be directed toward building the needed competence. The problem was in how they viewed their jobs.

The most powerful developer of top performers is job experience. Development occurs if managers are expected to continuously improve, question, and change. They are supposed to learn from their mistakes and find better ways to perform. In fact they are supposed to not only do their job better but find better jobs to do. They must question and challenge the purpose and existence of their own jobs. Top performers have to be in the business of rendering obsolete their own jobs and creating new and even more powerful jobs with more leverage and greater potential to the organization.

In Jacks's organization, executives and managers were hired, trained, and promoted to be work horses and do the job as defined. Traditional managerial competencies were rewarded, but within the narrow frame of getting the job done as defined. They were not expected to go beyond the job, to adjust and respond, to use new strategic competencies. New ideas and the errors that result from trying them out were not tolerated. Executives in Jacks's organization said, "Better not to take a risk than to take a risk and fail." The consequence was that they kept waiting for someone to tell them what to do. They made safe moves and produced predictable results. People do not perform to their maximum until they have tried and failed. If they are not allowed to fail, they will never confront and push back their limits. They never have a chance to push and develop their competence. If managers are to develop, they can not have strictly defined jobs. They must be able to create and recreate their own jobs. They must be allowed to push their own competence. They must be empowered.

We pointed out to Jacks that he did not have top performers because people were not learning from their experience. They hired excellent people who stopped learning the minute they reported to work. They were afraid to adjust and change. They were responsive to bureaucratic controls, not to customers and competition. They took no risks and concentrated only on those things they already knew how to do well. They never pushed themselves into new areas. Consequently, they never developed their own competencies. The roots of the company's problems lay with management, not with the employees.

We identified two objectives for Jacks and his executive group:

1. Hold each manager accountable for continuously improving and responding to customers and competition.
2. Hold each manager accountable for encouraging and helping employees to continuously improve their own strategic competencies.

This was a substantial shift in philosophy. The objective was to increase the availability of strategic skills. Enhancing on-the-job experience was the most efficient way to develop them. By focusing on developing skills through performing on the job, competencies would directly be related to what needed to be accomplished.

BUY TOP PERFORMERS

The third option you have to moving or developing top performers is to buy them. By this we mean hiring from the outside. We mention buying top performers last because it should be the last to consider. The grass always appears greener on the other side. Those from the outside will always look a little better than they actually are simply because you do not know them. Not only do you run risks of the unknown when you buy people from the outside, but they will be expensive. Other people want to keep their top performers. Also, you are going to have to give them good reasons to move: money, opportunity, ability to influence, or positions of authority. Those who are already in the corporation are going to have to be convinced it was worth the expense. Even with all the drawbacks it can be done, as Scully's move from Pepsi to Apple and Iacocca's move to Chrysler demonstrate.

DO NOT LET WEAKNESSES STOP YOU

As you focus on placing top performers into key positions, do not allow weaknesses to develop in other areas and prevent you from succeeding. Every area has minimum requirements which must be met for strategy to be successful. All too frequently, organizations do not succeed because of incompetence in small, seemingly insignificant areas. A new product is not introduced on time because an advertising manager did not get the promo-tional material necessary to support it ready on time. An important quality improvement system has no payoff because a manager in charge of the budget does not allocate money properly.

Arrowstreet, Inc., a firm of architects and planners, was highly sought after because of its ability to produce innovative designs. The prin-cipals were very talented in all aspects of building design. However, a bottleneck occurred when it came time to convert the innovative designs to construction blueprints. They simply did not have the talent to render their drawings into construction documents. While they had talented people in the critical area of design, they could not complete projects due to the lack of people with the necessary supporting skills. An aggressive recruiting and hiring program quickly addressed the problem.

IDENTIFY THE REAL
PERFORMANCE PROBLEM

As you assign people and build competence, you should understand and manage three common problems (see the performance matrix in Figure 4-1):

Problem #1: Doing the wrong thing wrong

Problem #2: Doing the wrong thing right

Problem #3: Doing the right thing wrong

Problem #1 is doing something that misses the market or goal and doing it poorly. The U.S. auto makers continued to produce big gas-guz-zlers after the demand for them dropped substantially (the wrong thing). Furthermore, the customer complaints indicated how poor the quality was (doing it wrong). Key performers will not help. You need to reexamine what you are doing.

Problem #2 is getting very good at doing the wrong thing. Key per-

FIGURE 4–1   Performance Matrix

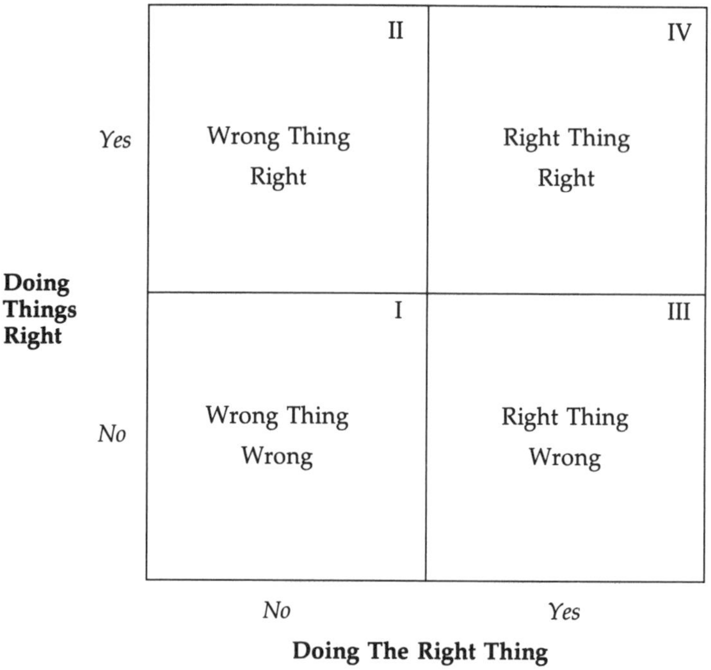

		II	IV
Yes		Wrong Thing Right	Right Thing Right
Doing Things Right		I	III
No		Wrong Thing Wrong	Right Thing Wrong
		No	*Yes*

Doing The Right Thing

formers will not help either. You must figure out the right thing to do. The seductive power of this mistake is that it hides problems until it's too late. For example, your firm may not be doing well, sales are down, and profits declining. The natural tendency is to push for increased productivity, cut costs, and motivate workers. Everyone will become energized and focused. Productivity may increase dramatically. Everything may appear to be working with systems in place and people working to top efficiency. The problem of course is that everyone and everything is focused in the wrong direction. They are working superbly producing the wrong product or delivering the wrong service. To avoid this mistake you must ask periodically if you are working on the right things.

A California company located in Silicon Valley specializing in the production of a sophisticated integrated circuit found its market taken away by producers of a new generation of integrated circuits (ICs). Faced with a dim future based on this new competitive threat, the leadership of the company decided to take action. High quality and low production costs became top priorities. They changed production methods but continued to do what they knew best—that is, make the old-generation ICs. The numbers of products meeting quality standards rose from 75 percent to 98 percent; production went from dozens of units per day to hundreds per day; and costs per circuit dropped by 50 percent. Thus, the company became a great producer of the wrong products. Customer demand had already shifted to the new-generation ICs, and nobody wanted their product, regardless of quality or price. Instead of working to develop new skills to produce new products, the company enhanced the old skills at producing old products. People want to do what they do well. They hang onto the familiar. Moving to new products and methods is threatening. Chapter 6 discusses how to deal with this problem.

Problem #3, doing the right thing wrong, is also a hard problem to manage. Check if you have the right people and skills in place. Be sure your key performers are positioned well. The tendency will be to give up and go back to areas in which you do better rather than stick with the new areas. We all fall back on what we are good at doing—even if it is the wrong thing. But the power of a good strategy is it keeps you focused on doing the right thing. Keep reinforcing strategy while looking carefully at what isn't working.

LEVERAGE TOP PERFORMERS

You have to get leverage out of people in your key positions. They are like booster stations in the television business. They take the signal and spread it over an area much broader than the original signal could have reached. Those holding key positions have a triple impact: (1) who holds the key positions will determine what skills will be brought to the job; (2) who is put in key positions sends a message concerning the type and level of performance needed, recognized, and promoted; (3) people in key positions will have a tremendous opportunity to learn and develop new skills from their jobs.

Consider Don Runkle's impact when he was the chief engineer for Chevrolet Motor Car Division in the mid-1980s. We as well as others knew Runkle as an aggressive engineer. He was outspoken almost to brashness, quick in decision making, and pushed others to keep up with him. He enjoyed learning "how to work the organization" and was known for working in and around the system to get things done. He skirted the edges of insubordination and worked as a scavenger, pulling resources from all over the organization to push his pet projects to completion. His boss at the time was Bob Burger, head of Chevrolet (now retired), who said, "Half the time you would like to strangle him, the other half you think he is brilliant." Runkle also loved cars and engines. He would rather have spent his time at the race track or state fair watching tractor-pulls than being in a staff meeting. Cars were in his blood.

Don Runkle's job required working with the central Chevrolet-Pontiac Canada (CPC) engineering organization. Runkle's responsibilities included coordinating Chevrolet's needs with those of the engineering department, and making sure CPC was designing and engineering cars that

Chevrolet customers wanted. No small task considering Runkle had no formal authority over the 10,000 people in CPC Engineering who did the work. Runkle also worked with the Chevrolet dealers, finding out their problems, obtaining marketing data, and coordinating their work with Engineering. Again, he had no formal authority, but had to get his work done through informal relationships, quick thinking, and fast moving.

The job was a good match for Runkle. He was a fine example of how to position people to pull strategy into results. Whether people liked or disliked Don Runkle, they admitted he cut through the bureaucracy and got things done. He was exactly the type of person necessary for a job with tremendous responsibility and no formal hierarchical authority, but nevertheless absolutely vital for making the organization work. Runkle's promotion sent a clear message about the type of people who would be promoted into these types of jobs, and it put Runkle in a position to develop managerial skills. For the first time he reported to a nonengineer, Bob Burger, head of Chevrolet. Burger, a salesperson, pushed Runkle to make engineering responsive to the market. Runkle expanded his skills. He made the CPC engineering organization more responsive to the market and brought a needed technical input into the sales organization. Proper positioning of the work force allows people development and strategy implementation to happen simultaneously.

We recently found another dramatic example of the impact of a key person's behavior at a consulting firm. One of the realities few consultants keep in mind is that consulting firms need managing too. In this case, the manager of the consulting group in a firm was himself an individual contributor. He was an excellent consultant and liked contact with clients. The quality of his work was top notch. However, the growth of the staff and business was poor. The indirect consequence of his being an excellent but autonomous individual contributor was that his staff also tended to perform as individual contributors and acted relatively independently of each other.

Without changing the reward system, or policies, or announcing any intended changes (he wanted his behavior to speak for itself), he redefined his main task as the development of his people and the formation of a cohesive unit. He pulled back gradually from project assignments and spent more time coaching (less billable time) and talking with his staff. Because each consultant kept careful record of how time was spent for charge-out purposes, we were able to track the impact of this change on his staff. Within a year we noted that those who reported directly to him reduced their billable time while increasing the time allocated to development and integration of their staffs. This multilevel change had several results: Revenues increased substantially as junior people stepped up to more senior-level work, and became more effective in selling. In addition, the unit became a much more satisfying place to work, with turnover cut from 33 percent to 5 percent in two years.

MANAGER'S CHECKLIST

1. Clearly identify how your unit or department adds value to the customer. If you do not directly deal with the customer, identify how you can help others who do directly serve the customer. Spend your next staff meeting figuring out how to give the customer even more "bang for their dollar spent." Then be sure you have your best people in positions that add the most value to the customer.

2. Identify your top performers and move them into key positions. Do not worry about tradition, organization protocol, or maintaining neat career paths. You are losing tremendous opportunities by not having your top performers in the key leverage positions. Move them.

3. Develop a list of skills you are learning from your job. If the list is not long enough, redesign your job so you can continue to learn. Now do the same for those who work for you. Hold everyone accountable for continuously improving their ability to perform on the job.

4. Make sure you understand the types of mistakes you are making. Doing the wrong thing right is far more serious than doing the right thing wrong. Working very hard and accomplishing the wrong thing may psychologically make you feel good, but the job does not get done. Constantly step back and ask yourself if you are going down the right path. In fact, a good friend can be very useful in helping you analyze what you are doing. Have them ask you the hard questions others are often hesitant to ask.

CHAPTER 5

Key #3: Unleash People's Potential

M ost people have far more potential than they use on their jobs. Systems, procedures, and managers get in their way. If work is not getting done, managers often assume people just do not have it in them. Their solution is to get new people. But often the best and quickest solution is to remove the constraints holding people back. People do not perform to their highest potential because managers limit them. For example, a few years back, during a trip from Detroit to Boston, as the second author boarded the plane another passenger recognized him and remembered that he had worked with the Technical Development Division (TDD) of Polysar, Ltd, eleven years earlier. Polysar is a worldwide manufacturer of synthetic rubber, latex, and chemicals based in Sarnia, Ontario, Canada. The stranger excitedly began explaining how in one year the division went from a demoralized, mediocre unit to a productive, high-energy unit. People who were low producers caught "fire" and became high producers.

What happened to cause the turnaround and why eleven years later was this manager excited to retell the story? Eleven years ago performance was poor, market share was declining, budgets and staff were cut to conserve money. Some key staff left. Those who remained had little self-respect and confidence.

Mark Abbott was appointed head of TDD and charged with turning it around. He inherited a unit considered a weak second cousin by other Polysar units. Employees of TDD viewed Mark with skepticism. How could an outsider, especially one from the Corporate Planning staff who knew little about their technology, possibly succeed?

Abbott began his tenure by voicing support for the people at TDD. He saw his role as building confidence and cutting back the bureaucracy so people could do their jobs. He spent much time out on the floor restating and asserting his confidence in people's ability to do their job and to achieve. He began a newsletter with the specific goal of broadcasting successes. This was not to be the typical whitewashed list of dull events, but rather a personal journal of individual and group achievements. Abbott wrote the newsletter himself and distributed it to all TDD employees.

Abbott had everyone discuss with their supervisors what they saw as their strengths, their job-related interests, and what was in the way of getting their job done. The purpose was to give employees a chance to structure their jobs or move themselves into jobs where they might perform more effectively. Twice a year, Abbott and his staff held a retreat to discuss what they as top management could do to help people improve their performance. Most importantly, and here is a key point, what could they stop doing to improve their performance? That is, what forms could be eliminated, what reports canceled, what meetings deleted? All in an effort to free people so they could focus their efforts on productive work.

The results were exciting. The level of communication within the division increased enormously. Rather than fighting each other and protecting turf, the senior staff began working together as a team. Abbott thrust responsibility to lower levels and held everyone accountable for making good business decisions that had payoffs in the marketplace. He did not recruit new people; he helped existing people increase their performance. The output of TDD in terms of innovations, new products, and problems solved skyrocketed. Within a year, TDD went from the division many were trying to get out of to the division many were trying to get into. Rather than considering themselves "losers," the people viewed themselves as "winners" and gained valuable experience which has served them well. Many have risen to top positions. The performance ethic that Abbott and the management team put in place continued well after the original team moved on. And eleven years later people were still telling the story of how great it was to finally be allowed to produce.

The Hansen Towers

Consider another example: George Hanks (all fictitious names) had high expectations when he took over the Hansen Towers redevelopment project in Houston, Texas. Hansen Towers was one of the biggest buildings in Houston and had enjoyed the image of being "the place to be." Most of the top real estate clients in the area had space in Hansen Towers. In the early 1980s, however, a glut of new construction challenged its prestigious position. A large insurance company purchased the building in 1985 and contracted Hanks to be the asset manager. There were some obvious problems with "The Tower," but none appeared insurmountable. Occupancy had slipped from 95 percent to 85 percent in six months. By Houston standards, the building was old and tired, but it still had many positive features and it was in a prime location. It was not too old to fix up for a minimal cost and many of the key tenants were still in the building. Considering the building's reputation and condition, George Hanks arrived anticipating that with minor cosmetic improvements, the building could be filled to capacity and become very profitable.

What he found was quite different. Arthur Andersen, as well as other major clients, left virtually as Hanks arrived. Rather than a 95 percent occupancy, by the time Hanks arrived on site, the building had only a 60 percent occupancy. Many of the major tenants whose leases were up for renewal indicated they would be leaving. In fact, many had already left, continuing to pay rent and not occupying their offices. The Houston market was turning soft; new buildings were going up and the economy was going down. Meanwhile, the building itself was in trouble. The heating and cooling systems were not functioning properly, tenant relations were at an all time low due to practices of the prior management team, and employee morale was dismal. Hanks and the management team faced a significantly greater challenge than anticipated.

After analyzing the market conditions, Hanks and the rest of management decided the best chance for survival was complete renovation of the building. Rather than spend a few hundred thousand dollars on paint and wallpaper, they proposed and the insurance company who owned the building agreed to spend roughly $30 million to completely renovate the electrical, heating, and cooling systems and give the building a major face-lift.

Once approval was given, the challenge was to turn the project around. The employees who had witnessed the decline now needed to help manage the turnaround. Hanks and the management team began a series of weekly meetings to keep the staff informed and to get them involved in the decision-making process. He gave them information about the project and anything that would help them do their job. Together, Hanks and his team established a schedule of renovation and a list of key priorities: (1) tenants, and (2) everyone else.

Not only did Hanks involve the staff, he held them accountable and responsible. The weekly staff meetings turned into problem-solving sessions where everyone worked together to solve their problems. What they discovered was that everyone was following the procedures and getting their job done but few employees were really worried about the client. What they did was limit the formal procedures and instead instituted a simple rule: If it helps the tenant, do it. Employees were involved and held accountable for meeting tenant needs. Surprising things began to happen when employees were included, made responsible, held accountable, and given the freedom to perform. Not only did the old employees change but they also made sure the new contractors brought in to help with the construction knew the tenant was number one.

Construction workers who used to dirty the elevators and leave debris strewn throughout the lobby began to clean up after themselves; they painted the scaffolding so it would not be unsightly; they entered and left through their own side door so as not to dirty tenant entrances.

Maintenance personnel started responding to tenant calls. "Hot" and "cold" calls had often been ignored or placed way down on the priority list. Now the new standard was to keep the temperature even at the right level. This was no simple challenge because construction called for removing windows, replacing doors, and changing elevators, all of which caused drastic swings in temperature inside the building.

The tip-off that things were "different" came one Friday afternoon when Leasing called Maintenance to inform them that trucks were waiting in the alley to unload furniture and equipment of a new tenant moving onto the twenty-third floor. This was the first Maintenance had heard of the new tenant. Construction had not been completed on the walls and floors, and the offices were in complete disarray. Workers who six months ago would have been yelling and screaming at each other, pitched in and worked all weekend. Walls were completed, flooring installed, and equipment moved. Maintenance worked with Construction, Leasing hauled boxes, and by Monday morning a very happy tenant, completely unaware of the weekend's close call, moved in to a newly decorated and renovated office space. There were no formal procedures, rules, or guidelines that could have accomplished the same result.

As the redevelopment project moved forward, Construction, Maintenance, and Leasing continued to yell and scream at each other. But now, as opposed to six months previously, the yelling and screaming involved plans to solve construction snags and make the systems work better, and how to cooperate, rather than assign blame or shift responsibility. Management had removed the constraints and the results were explosive.

As another example, in 1989 Ron Johnson, executive vice-president of PhotoMetrics, decided to change the basic assumption he had been making about the people working for him. Up until that point, he had seen his role as more of a protector and father to his subordinates directing their actions. In doing so, he realized he had been inadvertently holding back their performance. In February 1989, instead of sitting down weekly with his key subordinates and reviewing their plans and actions, he started to focus more on overall goals and objectives and using weekly sessions to find out what was getting in the way of employees performing on their job. The weekly sessions went from a very tightly scripted agenda to one where Johnson sat down with his employees with a blank sheet of paper, and asked them what was preventing them from getting their job done and how he could help.

Some months later, the volume of business at PhotoMetrics hit an all time high. This record performance continued through 1989 as Johnson's behavior built on the energy which already existed. One of Johnson's subordinates described the shift that had taken place. "I no longer have to spend all my time filling out forms and going to senseless meetings. I can now spend my time on getting the job done."

In turn, his subordinates mirrored the change in Johnson's behavior toward them in the way they treated the people reporting to them. It should be noted that what unleashed the energy here was not change in the reward system or business plans or strategy of the company; rather it was the change in top management's behavior. The focus of top management was on removing constraints. Ron Johnson's change allowed others' behavior to change and that in turn resulted in the change of behavior of key employees. An incentive system was put in place, not so much to spur the new behavior as much as to acknowledge it and make sure there was recognition for the anticipated good news at the end of the year. A hiring mechanism was established to bring on board talented employees to help sustain the growth. All because a manager decided to turn employees loose and see what they could accomplish.

In the case of TDD, Hansen Towers, and PhotoMetrics, the same people who had been spinning their wheels became highly effective. The difference was not the people; the difference was the way they were managed. In each case, the problem was not finding new talent, but removing the constraints and unleashing the potential already existing. We find in many situations the problem of energizing people is not a creation problem, not a question of bringing in new people; it is an unleashing problem—determining how to remove constraints so people can perform. Management's main questions to employees become:

- "What can I do to help you do your job more effectively?"
- "What can I do to reduce the time you waste?"
- "What can we take care of for you so that you can focus on your job?"

THE PETER PRINCIPLE IS WRONG

Laurence Peter has formulated what he refers to as the *Peter Principle* to explain organizational problems.[1] The Peter Principle states that people are promoted based on performance in their current job. They are promoted until they reach a job they cannot do. They remain there because they can no longer perform the job they are given. Because everyone eventually rises to the level of their incompetence, organizations are staffed by people who cannot do their job. Fortunately, the Peter Principle is wrong.

From our perspectives, several fallacies exist in the Peter Principle. It

---

[1]Laurence J. Peter, *The Peter Prescription*, (New York: William Morrow) 1972, p. 11.

assumes people's energy and ability is limited, especially their ability to learn and change. They progress until they hit their limit and then stop striving. Having hit the limit, they become complacent and accept their own low performance, with the rationalization that the job is beyond them. Fortunately, people do not have limits. They can always strive and improve; managers impose limits by their actions and systems.

Also inherent in the Peter Principle is a focus on making decisions based on past and present performance rather than on potential and future performance. People are promoted based on how well they are doing in the current job.

If you accept the Peter Principle, you assume a person who is not performing has reached his or her level of incompetence. Your only choice is to work around him because he or she cannot improve. We believe this orientation causes obvious problems. First, promotions and other management decisions are made based on ability to do past and present jobs, not ability to do future jobs. This approach is what causes many organizations to promote very good technicians to be very bad managers. Workers do not have expectations that developing and improving for future assignments are part of their current responsibilities. Second, managers do not receive any recognition for developing people unless it contributes to the immediate task.

Contrary to the Peter Principle we assume: (1) people can continually learn, and (2) management's job is to manage future and potential performance as well as present performance. These assumptions can provide substantial payoffs to the organization. The level of present performance increases because each person is motivated to do the job as it exists, to solve problems and to look for better ways to do the job, and they prepare for the job and challenges they will face in the future. Future performance also increases because employees are constantly striving to improve and prepare for the future.

If you assume people cannot learn and think, and thus rise to the level of their incompetence, you are constantly searching for new people who have the skills and motivation needed to replace people who have hit their limit. If you assume people can change, improve, and learn, you remove restraints and create conditions that allow workers to perform to their existing potential and develop increased potential. You should not focus on looking for extraordinary people, but rather on creating the conditions for ordinary people to do extraordinary things by removing the barriers preventing them from performing.

Focusing on potential and future performance does have risks. It requires a totally different management style than focusing on present performance. Figure 5-1 describes the differences in orientation. To manage present performance, managers must clearly define short-term goals, develop budgets, assign people to tasks, monitor results, and correct where necessary. If performance is low, it is justified by statements such as "we

FIGURE 5-1 ▪ Managing Present Performance versus Managing
               Potential and Future Performance

Present Performance	Potential and Future Performance
Define goals	Define goals
Control resources	Find resources
Select competent people	Develop people
Establish guidelines	Remove constraints
Measure and define skills	
	Measure and define potential
Monitor results	Redefine performance
Adjust performance	
	Provide training to improve performance

didn't have the right people," or "management didn't give us enough resources," or "we needed more time." All these reasons blame resource
constraints. Managing potential and future performance focuses on building competence to do the job now and in the future. Over the course of a
project, the goals and the paths to achieve them are constantly redefined
based on the increasing competence of the worker. Failure to achieve a
specific goal is not seen as overall failure. Failure happens because people
do not have the resources, or do not yet know how to perform. Mistakes
are teaching tools, not excuses for punishment. If performance is low over
a long period of time, it simply means a mismatch has occurred. The employee is in the wrong job, and at least 50 percent of the responsibility
belongs to management.

The tasks in Figure 5-1 listed under "Present Performance" are consistent with "getting the job done." They come from the "plan, control, do"
mentality of only looking at the work to be done. Planning how to do it,
establishing ways to measure progress, and then executing the work and
adjusting if problems arise are all part of this approach.

The tasks listed under "Potential and Future Performance" include
what appears in the first column to some extent. Goals have to be defined,
measures established, and performance adjusted. The difference is that the
measures and goals are used to develop and motivate performance rather
than to control it. The manager begins by working with the employee to
define the goals and measures. They identify what steps can be taken to
further build the skills necessary to do the job and to further the employee's career. The manager lets the employee focus on control while he
or she focuses on helping the employee develop. An important way a
manager can help the employee measure and define his or her development potential is by giving the employee regular, candid feedback on his or
her performance.

THE MANAGER/EMPLOYEE RELATIONSHIP

Focusing on removing the constraints to unleash potential creates the need to constantly redefine the manager/employee relationship. Relationships can be seen to go through four phases.

Phase I: Structuring Expectations and Responsibilities

In this phase the employee needs help defining job responsibilities and performance expectations. He or she needs help identifying what the task is and how to do the job. The focus is on doing the job as it is currently structured. The focus is on the present.

Phase II: Managing Linkages

In this phase the employee understands his or her specific job and now needs help understanding how this job relates to what others are doing. How is it connected to other jobs? The employee will need help managing relationships with others.

Phase III: Problem Solving and Conflict Resolution

After the employee understands the job and how it relates to others, he or she can begin anticipating problems and opportunities. The employee needs help managing proactively rather than simply reacting to situations. The employee anticipates and deals with conflicts.

Phase IV: Developing Potential

When the employee has mastered the job and can anticipate and prepare for the future, he or she is ready to push back constraints, increase personal potential, and expand ability. Now the employee needs help developing potential, changing the job, or moving on.

The problem, of course, for the manager is that as the employee becomes increasingly competent and accepts more responsibility, the manager feels less necessary. By the time the employee reaches Phase IV, the manager may feel no longer needed. The employee is doing it all. This, of course, is not the case. The manager need only shift his or her orientation. Instead of assuming his or her job is to duplicate (on a higher level) what the employee does, the manager should feel responsible for preparing for the future, representing the employee to the rest of the organization, and obtaining resources. The manager, under this definition, does what only he or she is uniquely qualified and positioned to do, that is, manage "up" the organization, coordinate across units, plan, and unleash the potential of people.

Guiding and developing employees to Phase IV will be psychologically threatening at first. Managers might feel out of control or out of contact. After all, bosses are supposed to be making decisions, telling people what to do, and monitoring results. In fact, a common reaction we find from bosses who have taken their employees to Phase IV is that they don't feel like the boss any more. A subtle shift has taken place. In Phase I it is clear the boss is in charge. He or she knows best how to do the job and manage the process of getting it done. The work flow comes from the boss at the hub and is disseminated out. He or she is like the surgeon, while nurses, technicians, and assistants stand ready to follow his or her explicit instructions. (See Figure 5-2.)

In the traditional manager/employee relationship, the employees all concentrate on what the manager directs them to do. The limit to their performance can easily become the limits of the manager in assigning and directing the work. The unleashed relationship has the manager directed toward the employees so he or she can listen to them for what he or she can do to help improve their performance.

Over the course of the second and third phases, the employees learn how to manage the tasks and become technical experts. Then they learn how to work with others to coordinate their accomplishments. The manager becomes less and less the center of communications and decisions.

In Phase IV the work gets done outside the manager's circle. Suddenly, the manager is working for the employees. They have the expertise, they are directing the work flow, and the manager's function has shifted to that of coordinator, communicator, and representative.

As long as a manager is the center of the work, he or she is the limit. The group can do no more than the manager's ability allows them. If the employees become the center of the work, the limit is greatly expanded.

FIGURE 5-2 • Superior/Subordinate Relationship

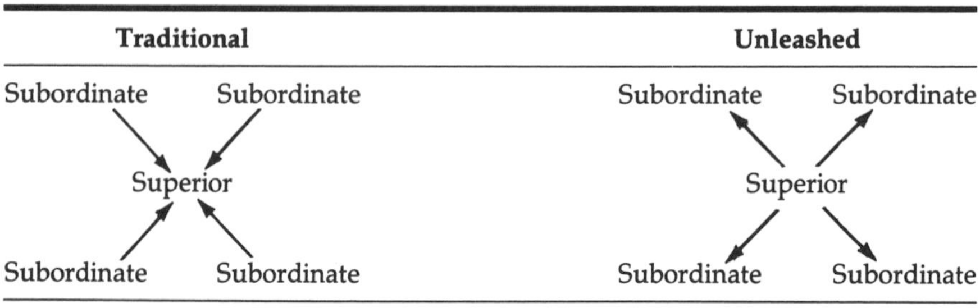

This is the principle Mark Abbott, George Hanks, and Ron Johnson tapped into, and thus unleashed the potential of their people. We are not arguing that present performance should be ignored because it cannot be. We are arguing that both present and future performance must be measured and managed simultaneously. The measures of present performance are important because they are the basis for day-to-day judgments. However, without the measures of future performance, managers are rewarded solely for consuming resources and producing short-term results, not building and preparing for the future.

THE TWO APPROACHES

Managing future performance sets up a very different dynamic than managing present performance. When focusing on present performance, managers work with employees by carefully defining what needs to be done, selecting employees who have the skills to do the job, communicating performance expectations clearly, measuring performance, and rewarding based on what is accomplished. Employees do the job exactly as defined. This approach sets up dynamics which limit performance. A self-fulfilling prophecy is established. Employees are expected to do what has already been defined and that is the limit of what they will do. They do not go beyond because beyond has not been defined and there is no reward for going there.

When focusing on future performance, managers work with people by providing opportunities for employees to push back the limits, by assigning responsibility for success and failure, and by allowing employees the experience necessary to increase competence. With this approach, employees look for new challenges, take risks, and expand their capabilities. This approach also sets up a self-fulfilling prophecy. If the reasons for working are to succeed, accomplish, and learn, employees are more likely to succeed, accomplish, and learn.

Admittedly, this portrayal is overly black and white. Most managers do not focus exclusively on either present or future performance. We describe them in extreme terms to make the point that your approach as a manager will cause employees to behave in certain ways.

Of course, you must manage both present and future performance and maintain a balance between them. The balance is crucial; problems can arise if you focus too much on either present or future performance. Each imbalance creates unique problems. If you focus too much on present performance, you will frustrate employees who already know how to do the job and manage their relationships with others. They are ready to increase their ability, change the job to improve performance, and push back the constraints. They need a Phase IV relationship and you insist on managing them in Phase I. You spend a great deal of time defining performance expectations and making sure they understand and focus on doing the job the way it is defined. You may be able to convince them to perform the job exactly as defined, but you will not get any extra effort. They are more likely to withdraw than innovate or achieve their potential. You will never know how far they could have gone.

The opposite is the case if you focus too much on pushing potential. Assume your employees need a Phase I relationship with structured expectations and clear definitions of the job. If you push them to increase their ability, be innovative, redefine the job to increase performance, and anticipate and prepare for future opportunities and problems, you will only confuse and debilitate them. You have gone too far, too fast. It's time to slow down, cycle back to the first phase.

In order to determine what phase employees are in, the manager must accurately assess performance. Employees in Phase I will be doing the task assigned without planning, innovating, or anticipating changes. Employees in Phase II will be able to plan their work and identify how their job interrelates with others. They will recognize the interdependencies between their work and that of others. In Phase III, innovation and initiation of changes that reflect an understanding of the system of activities will be possible. Employees in Phase IV will be looking to redefine the job in order to improve performance and develop their capabilities.

Movement from one phase to the next can be best done after employees have developed the skills necessary to perform well in the previous phase. Expectations of the phases and steps for progressing from one phase to the next need to be defined in advance with employees. These expectations include: (1) what the steps are to and through each phase, (2) the responsibilities of the manager and employees for moving employees ahead, (3) how progress will be seen, and (4) the goals of the development. Trying to move employees without this understanding and commitment will make the process much more difficult.

THE ENVIRONMENTAL CREATOR

When you focus on unleashing potential, you assume people not only do the job, but they learn from doing the job. They not only master the skills necessary, but they learn new ways to accomplish the job and improve the way it is done. Studies on adult learners indicate that the best way to learn is from experience and that people are their own best teachers. You cannot learn your students, they learn for themselves. Your job is to construct the environment so they have the maximum potential to learn.

The role of the manager striving to manage potential is not that of a hands-on manager who gets overinvolved in the details, but that of "environmental creator." In many situations management is the constraint, not the employee. The concept is simple. Give them the tools and get out of their way. If poor-quality products are being produced, help them change the system by which the products are designed. Change the resources available; change the working relationships of people doing the jobs. If projects consistently overrun the budget, change the planning process, or change the management process. Make changes in the employees' work environment. Expect high performance, but give the employees an opportunity to both succeed and fail. You manage the environment, they do the work. If your focus is present performance, you will be tempted to introduce more controls if people fail. Inspectors, checkers, coordinators, and expeditors are positioned to more closely measure, monitor, and control. However, if you are managing potential, you will make those doing the job responsible for finding out what went wrong and determining how to fix it.

Consider what happened in the General Motors-Toyota joint venture in Fremont, California. Prior to the joint venture, the Fremont plant had one of the poorest quality, productivity, and on-time records in GM; and in March 1982, it was closed. Five thousand hourly workers were let go and General Motors was sitting on an aged, vacant, 200-acre plant complex. In early 1984 Fremont was reopened under a joint GM-Toyota agreement to produce small cars. Under this agreement GM provided the plant, the Japanese provided the management staff, philosophy, and techniques. Twenty-five hundred workers were carefully screened and rehired and the plant once again went into production. Over the next year, that same plant and a number of employees from the same work force received some of the highest ratings in the GM system. They went from the worst to the best in a very short period of time.

The difference was not massive infusions of new technology, a new work force, or modern facilities; the difference was in management practices. The best example of the difference was the problem-solving groups and the *stop line* installed on the production line. The 2,500 employees, all informally titled *problem-solving managers,* were divided into teams of five to eight, with each team responsible for managing their work and solving production and quality problems. The stop line was a simple technology change: A rope was installed that workers could pull to stop the production line.

The stop line was a radical change in management philosophy. To keep the line moving is the first and most important job of any General Motors plant management. At the Fremont plant, however, hourly workers have the ability and authority to stop the line any time they see a problem. The rules, the organization, and the philosophy have been changed. The employees are no longer controlled by the assembly line, they are in control of the assembly line. They are no longer considered elements in the process, but rather controllers of the process. They have been given the tools and are expected to solve the problems. Their job is not only to produce cars according to specifications, but to improve the process, anticipate and solve future problems, and improve production. Underlying all these changes was a belief in the potential of the people to continuously improve and strive for perfection. Workers were responsible for constantly improving their performance. Imagine the type of environment this creates. Management gave the responsibility to the workers and allowed them to perform. Management was the constraint, not the workers.

The same employees who produced the lowest-quality cars at GM produced the highest-quality cars because management removed the constraints, put control in their hands, and held them accountable. The potential was always there, but it took a plant closing and a new venture to release it.

GUIDING THE MISSILE

This is not to suggest you remove constraints by turning people loose to do whatever they want. Turn them loose to manage themselves to perform. As one Chief Executive Officer said, "We do not want loose cannons on the deck." Employees must be able to guide themselves. They must have a clear understanding of the target, they must have access to current information and feedback on how they are doing, and they must have the ability to adjust and correct. The key is accurate on-line information. This is the basis of the famed Kanban method of the Japanese. Timely information to the employee is seen as the best way for the employee to control the process. On a minute-by-minute basis, the employee can check for deviations. The employee who can make corrections is the one who gets the information. The flow of information to all employees not only gives them the ability to control the operation, it also promotes continuous improvement.

It works in the American culture also. For example, at Hansen Towers, everyone receives reports on occupancy rates, schedules for construction, information about new tenants and expected arrival dates. Never again will a tenant show up to occupy space that is not ready or requires a weekend of feverish preparation. This is not because activity has slowed down, but because that hectic weekend prompted the team to sit down and determine ways to prevent such disasters from happening again. The solution is to keep everyone informed regarding everyone else's activities. Each group issues weekly reports to all the others. Coordination meetings are held by each group to keep the other groups informed of their schedule. Everyone knows everyone else's schedule through the reports and coordination meetings. They no longer rely on top management to coordinate them; they coordinate and manage themselves.

A test of whether employees have power to guide themselves is what happens when their efforts are not successful. Missiles that go off track are blown up. People who go off track should be held accountable, given information, and allowed to get back on track.

Consider the following example: The Kendall Company, then a division of Colgate-Palmolive, needed to acquire a source of inexpensive gauze. The most likely source was the Far East with its cheap labor base. After three deals fell through, the company still actively supported the General Manager, and he set out to try again. No one was punished because the first three deals did not come through for one reason or another. Rather, they learned from their experience, sought out and were better prepared for the next opportunity. In 1987, a joint venture to produce gauze was successfully completed. Management in the Far East Division gained information and experience with each prior attempt and were able to analyze and determine where they went wrong. They had enough control to make corrections and try again.

The payoffs for involving employees and making them responsible for keeping themselves on track are visible and come quickly. In the case of Hansen Towers, it meant the difference between 60 percent occupancy with satisfied tenants, and 90 percent occupancy with satisfied tenants. In the case of GM's joint venture, it meant the difference between producing products with quality measures at 75 percent and quality measures at 98 percent.

MANAGER'S CHECKLIST

1. Next time you sit down with one of your employees to plan performance ask the three unleashing questions:
   a. What can I do to help you do your job more effectively?
   b. What can I do to reduce the time you waste?
   c. What can we take care of for you so that you can focus on your job?
2. Have your employees design their jobs so they can continually learn. Include new assignments that require employees to enhance their skills. Have them work with others from whom they can learn.
3. As you begin working with someone for the first time, make sure you structure expectations properly. In other words, what are your responsibilities and what are their responsibilities? Then make sure you both understand how the subordinate's job fits with others in the organization. Help the employee define and manage linkages critical for his or her performance.
4. Realize a large component of your job is managing up the organization. Develop a list of specific activities you can do tomorrow and next week to effectively manage "up" the organization.
5. Make sure your employees have timely information they can use to monitor and manage themselves. Do not flood them with information; give them information that is specific to their job.

Key #4: Build a Sense
of Action and Urgency

Neither crisis nor opportunity will move employees to action: They only create the necessary conditions. Unleashing people's potential to deal with crisis will do no good at all unless they mobilize their actions in the right direction. How employees respond (for example, with apathy, with action but in the wrong direction, or with purposeful action) depends on their perceptions of the situation. Most people want to believe all is well and what they are doing is good. They do not want to be told they are on the wrong track and/or they are not going fast enough. This simple observation lies at the root of why organizations with highly talented, well-positioned people, and above-average chances for success often fail. Opportunities are lost because of complacency. Competition and crisis may be threatening the very existence of the organization, but if employees do not see the threat, they will continue to carry on as usual. If employees are working hard but in the wrong direction, at least you have something to work with. Get them pointed in the right direction and they should produce solid business results. If they are apathetic there is no base on which to build. It is the managers, not the situation, who build the sense of action and urgency that focuses energy and produces solid business results.

A computer software company outside of Boston provides an example of what happens if people do not have a sense of urgency. The company was in terrible financial shape and steadily losing market share. So the old management was shuffled out and new management brought in; however, nothing changed. New lines of credit were secured, new marketing plans developed, and severe budget constraints imposed; still, nothing changed. Though employees gradually shifted their attention from low-priority to high-priority projects, they did not believe any crisis existed and thought they could just make changes as opportunities arose. A few years later the company declared bankruptcy.

The irony was that the company had good people. They even had them positioned correctly. However, the company's management did not build the sense of urgency necessary to prevent a business failure, so the employees continued to believe all was well. The crisis created conditions for action, but management did not use the crisis to initiate a sense of urgency that could have saved the company. After bankruptcy, new management restructured the company. Within two years the company had turned around, largely because the new managers were able to convince employees new directions had to be taken quickly. The irony was that they had used the plans developed by the previous managers. The missing ingredient was employee enthusiasm and motivation.

We can cite many examples from both large and small companies where the sense of urgency demanded by the situation did not exist. For example, deregulation forced life insurance companies into competition with banks and investment firms. Yet even today, many still have not developed financial service products that would make them competitive and the ones that have are not implementing them fast enough. The American automobile industry has known for a long time that they were in trouble, and they are slowly responding to their competitive challenge—maybe too slowly.

WHY DON'T PEOPLE ACT?

If getting people to pick up speed or to shift directions when a crisis exists is difficult, it is almost impossible to convince them to take advantage of a new opportunity, to implement plans avoiding losses in the future, or to make improvements in quality when the current product is selling well. There is no pain, so why search for a remedy? Why does this happen? Why don't people act? Why do they sit mired in their old ways even when it is obviously in their own best interest to change?

Individuals Prefer Stability and Continuity

For decades psychologists have studied people's unwillingness to change, even in the face of disaster, and have concluded that people find change psychologically threatening. We like stability and predictability, everything in its proper place. We enter an elevator and stand in the same corner, we sit in the same place in the lunch room, we park our car in the same spot in the lot, and we arrange our desks the same way every day. At the start of a semester, students choose seats and then take that seat every day. Why? Because changes cause uncertainty. Change is threatening. People want predictable routines. A basic law of physics states that a body in motion will continue on its path unless an outside force exerts pressures on it. This law also applies to people. People will continue doing what they are doing until an outside force exerts pressure on them.

If you don't believe change is threatening and people are emotionally involved with their parking spaces or seating places, vary the parking or seating rules. If parking is in designated places, make it first come, first served. If parking is first come, first served, then assign places. It does not matter how, just change the rules so they are different. Committees will form, suggestion boxes will be stuffed, and managers' ears will be ringing, even though employees will admit that where they park does not really matter. Where people park has very little to do with productivity and market success; it simply is not important. People will make it important because of their concern for status, relationships, security and predictability, and their concerns will affect how they act and what they accomplish.

If getting people to park or sit in a different place is threatening, imagine how threatening it is to be told the work you are doing is not delivering business results. What you are doing is too late, too slow, or completely wrong. People would rather continue what they are doing than change and adapt to new situations. Some people find it easier to avoid the whole issue by denying it exists. Others may admit change is happening but rationalize that it will only affect other people.

Fragmented Responsibility

The individual psyche is not the only source of inertia. The organization structure itself, which organizes people into departments, fragments the sense of responsibility for overall goals. Employees' primary focus is often on their department's goals, not on the organization's goals. This fragmented responsibility leaves few feeling responsible for the success of the whole organization. If there is no overall powerful coordinating mechanism, each department will go its own way.

For example, and we exaggerate here to illustrate our point, the Marketing Department will do marketing.[1] Their view of heaven is high-quality products, all shapes and all colors, unlimited flexibility and inventory, low prices, special incentives, extended credit terms, and large advertising budgets. If you don't like blue, take red. Special orders are no problem: Sure that model is in stock; I can have it here tomorrow. Marketing people focus on the peculiar interests of the customers and are always preparing to respond as these customers continually change their minds.

The Finance Department will focus on finance and control. Their view of heaven is no inventory, cash sales, low costs, no financing, and high prices. Better yet, let's sell products we have not yet made. Get customers

---

[1]For a full explanation of this phenomenon, see George Labovitz, *Managing For Productivity* (Burlington, MA: Organization Dynamics Inc., 1991), pp. 7–13.

to pay up front, take their cash to buy the raw materials and produce the product they want. Finance lives in a world of costs and profits, where expenses must be controlled and fluctuations in interest rates mean the difference between bankruptcy and success.

The Production Department is concerned with meeting schedules and cost and quality targets. Production people want virtually unlimited stocks of supplies, qualified workers, modern technology, predictable demand, and no interruptions for special orders. They want one shape, one size, one configuration so they can switch on the production line and let it run forever. Production lives in a world where costs and schedules reign supreme—costs and schedules obtainable by limiting the variety of products made.

Why don't people understand? They do not understand because they are buried in their own problems. Interactive Systems, Inc. (a fictitious name), a once very successful manufacturer of electrical components for word processors, struggled with a problem of low profit for twelve months. The president, Ed O'Brien, asked the vice-president of each of the four functional areas—Marketing, Engineering, Manufacturing, and Human Resources—to report back to him on what could be done to meet the profitability targets. While a number of factors undoubtedly contributed to the problem, he asked each of the vice-presidents to identify the number one priority problem throughout the company causing the lower profitability.

Four weeks later, O'Brien received four carefully documented reports. The report from the head of Marketing identified the number one priority problem as a lack of understanding of customer needs. He indicated that Engineering designed parts so they were more difficult to use and included materials which went beyond customer requirements. He pointed out that competitors were staying in close touch with customers and designing simpler parts that could be sold more cheaply. A number of Japanese firms were identified in the report as making serious inroads in Interactive's markets. The marketing report recommended an increase in sales force to maintain contact with customers, an increase in expenditures for market research, and better cooperation between the Marketing and Engineering departments in the design of new parts.

The vice-president of Engineering cited the number one contributor to low profitability was the difficulty of incorporating new technology into the products. He indicated that they were selling in a market where competition was based on technological advancements in microcircuitry. He pointed out the difficulty of staying in the lead was due to the tremendous advances made by competition who had made massive investments in R&D organizations. His report showed that the companies investing more in R&D as a percentage of sales were also those increasing their market share over Interactive Systems, Inc. His recommendation was a larger engineering budget including a microelectronics lab.

The vice-president of Manufacturing identified the issue as the con-

tinually increasing manufacturing costs. As a result, the differential between Interactive and other companies in processing costs had turned un-
favorable. He identified several reasons. First, the product was too
complex with too many parts. This unnecessarily increased manufacturing
costs. Second, he thought the engineering organization did not support
operations and, as a result, the production process was not sufficiently
well designed to minimize either the downtime of the machines or labor
costs. His recommendations included more carefully designed products
and better technical support for the Manufacturing Department.

The vice-president of Human Resources identified that the number
one problem was that the people in the organization were not motivated to
superior performance. She pointed out that the compensation plan of Interactive Systems was only average for those in the industry. She indicated
that there was a need for more involvement of the employees in management decision making. Her recommendations included revamping the
compensation system and launching an employee involvement campaign
similar to the quality circles other companies in the industry had tried.

O'Brien read each report carefully. Each provided good reasons and
documentation as to why theirs was the high-priority problem. The problem was that they were all right, from their fragmented perspectives, but
no one was thinking about the business. It was their functional bias and
their different views of the business, O'Brien decided, which were causing
the most serious problems. Unfortunately, this story may sound all too
familiar. It could have been written about many organizations, probably
even yours.

The problem is that the combination of fragmented responsibility and
divergent focus creates a situation where nobody "owns" progress towards
the overall goal. Marketing does marketing, Finance does finance, and
Production does production. Therein lies the problem. No one does business. Commitments are to the department, not to the organization. A serious situation requiring action by the company will not give the same
sense of urgency as a threat to personal or departmental goals.

Staff Advisors

Staff groups such as corporate financial staff, planning, or market research
departments also reinforce the tendency toward the status quo, inaction,
and slow movement. They provide expert advice and counsel but are neither decision makers nor implementors. Thus, they accept no responsibility for action. Having offered recommendations, they have fulfilled
their obligations. If others haven't taken heed of their expert advice, staff
cannot be blamed.

The staff's natural tendency is to analyze well beyond what is needed.
That is their job. Faced with a problem, they analyze and investigate the
costs and benefits of different alternatives. Because they do not have to

actually make and implement decisions, they want to make sure that those who do have as much information as possible. They avoid definitive answers and prefer to speak in terms of options: On the one hand we can do this, on the other hand we could do that; here is the cost/benefit of this and there is the cost/benefit of that. As Harry Truman once said after a briefing from a staff of economists, "What we need around here is a good one-handed economist."

Top executives often collude with staff inaction by requesting analysis and recommendations without action and implementation plans. Management not only allows but also expects the staff to submit reports analyzing a problem without providing actions or being responsible for implementation procedures. To let them go further would allow them to invade management turf. Staff exists to recommend, management exists to decide.

An excellent manager will not accept reports and recommendations without action and implementation plans. He or she will not allow presentations without assignments. Nobody leaves the room until follow-up actions are specified with deadlines attached. Similarly, an excellent staff will not make recommendations without action plans and steps forward. They will not leave meetings without pushing for specific assignments for action.

Consultants often make matters worse. Consultants serve as staff to the staff; thus, they are two steps removed from action. Consultants are paid to give advice. Most have no natural reason or motivation to implement recommendations.

Jack Rahaim, a senior technology manager in artificial intelligence for Digital Equipment Corporation, puts it this way:[2]

> People are always waiting for things to slow down. They always want less confusion. They talk about when the reorganization is over, or when the market settles down, or when the product priorities become clear. They long for the good old days when things were stable. Those days are gone forever. Don't wait for things to settle down. When the organization stops changing and moving, we should start asking questions. Something is wrong. Constant urgency, action, movement, reorganization, and new challenges are what business should be. If things stop and freeze, we are doing something wrong. We are competing against people that are not stopping. Sure we need to do good analysis. But analysis has its payoff in action. The best plan in the world is worse than a half-baked one that moves us forward. We may even make some bad decisions and wrong moves. That is OK because the only way we will know if they are bad is to make them. The magic of management is learning from mistakes, adjusting and changing quickly. You have to keep moving.

---

[2]Based on personal conversation, quoted with permission.

We find that good managers create a pull for purposeful action. They excite people by describing challenges in graphic terms while simultaneously providing direction and enthusiasm.

BE PREPARED TO MANAGE DENIAL AND RESISTANCE

Denial and resistance are natural responses to your requests for action. To effectively drive to action, you need to realize people will usually go through these stages before they are ready to move. You need to understand why people are denying and resisting. You are much better off helping people through these stages than ignoring them.

Consider the following conversation between a vice-president and a key middle manager of a U.S. manufacturing giant.

VICE-PRESIDENT: The changes announced by the President are out. Have you seen them? The whole organization is affected.

MIDDLE MANAGER: But we are losing the market because of our products, not our organization. Now we're so screwed up we'll be lucky if we even get new products out the door.

VP: The new structure is designed to improve communication so we can better understand our customers and get all parts of the organization closer to the market. Didn't you see the new charts?

MM: Sure, I saw the new charts, but you and I both know it's not structure but the people that make the difference—and the same people are in charge. Only it's worse because we used to know how to communicate and now we have to learn how to make the system work all over again.

VP: Come on. It used to take us weeks to make minor decisions and months to do anything important. Things weren't all that great. I used to listen to you complain about them all the time. This new structure gives us a chance to change all that, but we've got to get moving—we've already lost a lot of time.

MM: Time! It will take a lot more than just time. I haven't even had a chance to talk to anyone around here about this. As bad as the old organization was, at least I knew who to talk to and how to make it work. Now I don't know the players *or* the rules of the game.

VP: But the old structure was incredibly bureaucratic and ineffective. It wasted enormous amounts of everybody's time to make it work. Besides, the implementation workshops start on Friday and we'll all have a chance to see how it will work then.

MM: But they haven't changed the people, only the boxes. If they were serious they would have used this opportunity to get rid of some of the deadwood. Then at least we would see *some* positive change out of this thing.

VP: How many changes do you think we could take in a single week? I can see you are angry about this thing, but don't be foolish.

MM: Well I am angry. Who wouldn't be? It's a lot easier for you to see the silver lining in this thing. My only point is this: Sure, we had a lot of problems, sure we needed some changes. You're right. I've said for months that a real shake up was necessary and I'll even admit that *some* of the changes will be positive–in the long run. But do you know how difficult this new organization is going to be for me? Do you know how much time is going to be lost before I can get back to the point where I was only last week? It's guys like me who are going to pay the price for the incompetence of this company's leadership.

VP: I suppose you're right, but if we don't get off on the right foot–and fast–we'll be in even worse shape.

The vice-president is as impatient as his subordinate is frustrated. He wants to get on with the new organization, wants it implemented quickly, and sees the past only in the worst possible terms. The past is something to forget, to move away from. Its defects provide an easy justification for the changes, no matter how sweeping or difficult they will be for others. He has no time to listen to past problems or to understand that there will be more inefficiency and disorganization before things will get better. He does not want to hear about anything that will distract the firm from the tasks that lie ahead. For him this is not the time to dwell on the past, but the time to usher in the future. He seems to be telling his subordinate, "If you can't get on board now, the train will leave the station without you." He is not prepared to deal with the resistance most of his subordinates have. He most likely will be very surprised at how unwilling they will be to start implementing the new organization. He is building a sense of resistance rather than a sense of action and urgency.

People usually move through this normal sequence: denying the need to change (denial), being angry that they must do something different (anger), accepting the need to change but seeing it mainly as the responsibility of others (rationalization), and to finally understanding the need and accepting the responsibility for making it happen (acceptance). Figure 6–1 presents quotes from people at each of these stages. Only by carefully listening can a manager understand in which of these stages employees are functioning and how to help them move to the next level.

Managing Denial and Resistance

Effectively managing denial and resistance requires both an understanding of where people are and how they move through the stages and accept responsibility for action. Building a sense of urgency and an acceptance of the responsibility for action is largely a process during which the individuals must understand the old ways are not good enough and that they have a stake in making them better.

FIGURE 6-1 ▪ Varieties of Reactions to a Problem or Threat*

Denial that a problem or threat exists

- "We are not blind to the Japanese, if we were no one would buy our cars." (engineer at a U.S. automobile manufacturer)
- "Nothing will change here, we are a bunch of hard-working employees. I can't believe we are in trouble." (staff person at a software company fighting bankruptcy)
- "We have more technology in our storehouse than most companies ever see; we are in fine shape." (chemical company VP after its fifth year of poor performance)

Anger that there is a problem or threat

- "Management makes the mistakes, but we pay the price." (middle manager at a chemical company)
- "I have worked here for 30 years and loved every day of it. Now I don't. I don't look forward to coming to work anymore." (executive at an engineering firm)
- "All we do is have meetings, nothing gets done, nothing *will* get done. We are so screwed up. The managers don't know what they are doing." (manager at a hospital products company)

Rationalization; action may be necessary for others

- "When the others get their basics in place it will be O.K. Then I will try some different things." (planner at a retail organization)
- "They needed to do something. This reorganization was as good as anything." (engineer at an aerospace company)
- "There are a lot of managers who will hang on to their old ways but a new organization is necessary if we are going to be successful." (bank executive)

Resignation that action is unavoidable; accepting the inevitable

- "The change had to occur; we were fat, content, and sloppy." (executive of a large engineering firm)
- "Those S.O.B.s [the competition] have us. We'll show them." (engineer in an electronics manufacturer)
- "Change is unavoidable. Let's get on with it." (staff person in a bank)
- "Management really means it this time. Look at what they're doing." (middle manager in a consumer goods producer)

---

*These are actual quotes from the employees of companies under competitive threat. They are from interviews done by Frohman Associates as part of our consulting to help the companies successfully deal with the process of change.

Change thrusts people into uncertainty and the unknown. They will have questions. How will these new efforts affect me personally? Will I have to work harder? How long will this major push last? Although it is difficult to deal with these questions, people will never give you their wholehearted support until they are answered. If there is no opportunity for their questions to be aired, employees will remain skeptical and adopt a wait-and-see attitude that acts like a lead weight on any attempts to move to purposeful action.

Managers usually feel compelled to press immediately for full-scale, rapid action. They understand the pressures. Certainly everyone else just needs to be told what to do and they will be willing to go along. The following are reactions we have heard from members of diverse organizations who have experienced this traditional (and frustrating) implementation strategy.

- "I'm tired of being talked to. I want my manager to sit down with me and help me to understand what is happening."
- "No more videotapes or meetings. I need someone to listen to me."
- "Lots of workshops with donuts and coffee. Are they afraid to sit down one to one?"
- "My boss is too busy with all the meetings about the change. He is too busy to help me with my job."
- "All I see are videos. I hear what they say but I do not know what we are doing. There is no way for me to have input."
- "Don't pretend that you're a humanist and then just pay lip service to it."
- "We do not need more off-sites. We need more insights."

Let us return to the dialogue between the vice-president and middle manager and adjust it to show a different and more effective way of dealing with the middle manager's concerns.

VICE-PRESIDENT: The changes announced by the President are out. Have you seen them? It looks like we are in for some major changes.

MIDDLE MANAGER: I can't even understand what they are. It looks to me like they've thrown the whole organization up against the wall to see where the pieces would stick. And they thought we *used* to have problems. Give us a month and this will make the old structure seem streamlined and efficient. I can't believe they're serious about this, maybe this is just the trial balloon?

VP: No, really, I think they're perfectly serious. They may not be realistic about how fast it's going to work, but I think they are serious about wanting to do it.

MM: I can't even think about implementation now. All I can think about is how much *worse* this place will get. I can't believe they're doing anything this stupid—now—of all times.

VP: I understand what you are saying. The timing doesn't seem great and we probably will lose a lot of momentum before we get things on track again. It's going to take a lot of effort. Frankly, I'm worried that a lot of people won't be up for the work ahead.

MM: And I don't even know anything about my new section leader or the people in my department. Did they tell you?

VP: They haven't told me a whole lot about who is doing what in the new structure, except at the vice-president level. Actually, it's hard for me to focus much on that now. I'm concerned about all the projects we have up in the air. It seems like we accomplished a lot over the past two years. There ought to be some way to use it.

MM: You're right. We did do a lot together. It seems a shame to let it get lost in this new shuffle. It's just like this corporation: they have no memory. What's past is past, only what you're going to do tomorrow is important. But that's not going to change.

VP: But what we did is *still* important. We've learned a lot together—and we accomplished a lot. That counts for something and we need to think about what to do with it.

The vice-president does not attempt to deny the anger or the frustration of his subordinate. The reality is that life will be more difficult and precious time and energy will be spent figuring out how to make the new organization work. The old organization had many problems but at least it was familiar; people knew how to work in it. These are simple truths both managers understand. Both also seem to understand that their group made valuable contributions that may be at risk in the reorganization process. The vice-president wisely listens as he moves his staff toward implementation.

The irony implicit in moving to action is that there is more power in listening than there is in talking. Understanding that employees will resist and helping them through this stage are more important than applying more pressure.

The focus of implementation in many organizations is on making the new structure and systems fit the new strategy and on working through the implementation process in a rational, efficient way. The problem of implementation is often viewed as a need to work out the mechanics of the new organization, educating staff as to how the new structure works and giving people the information and tools they need to do their work effectively in the new environment. This approach assumes that what people need is the *means* to get the job done. Interventions focus on sharing information, understanding roles and responsibilities, sharpening up job descriptions, figuring out the decision-making process (who has the power) and learning how to communicate effectively in the new structure (influencing the power). Often as not, however, it runs into many problems and difficulties that do not respond to the traditional balm of sharing information and learning the new way of doing business. The problem is that it deals only with the second half of the change process, that is, retooling and sharpening one's ability to be effective in a new situation. It is silent on the first part of the process, the acceptance of change, and the initial reaction to a threat and desire to maintain the status quo.

Implications for Managers

Managing the early stages of moving to action challenges even the most seasoned and resourceful manager. Both traditional organizational development techniques and the results-oriented style of management can increase hostility and mistrust and push the implementation calendar even further behind.

We have several recommendations for managers who are having difficulties moving the organization to action. Although each of these by itself will not work miracles, as part of a larger and somewhat longer process, they can provide the necessary signals and tools to buffer these difficult times, reduce wasted effort, move closer to the time of normalcy, and return to the fundamental work of the organization.

1. *Analyze the current situation for the readiness to deal with all stages of action.* The organization, its leadership, and key managers must be ready and able to undertake a period of uncertainty and confusion marked by denial, anger, and rationalization. Rarely is the ability to implement a major corporate decision affected so directly by the emotional health and personal well-being of its managers. The better the emotional health of the individual, the better able he or she will be able to handle the change. Self-confidence, a sense of security and well-being, and a solid support network contribute to the ability of the organization's managers to implement changes of major proportions. An organization that is under great pressure or has gone through numerous changes is less likely to respond effectively and thoughtfully to the varieties of reactions that we have observed. Yet it is often when organizations feel most beleaguered and desperate that a renewed commitment to action is required.

2. *Develop a strategy for implementation that takes into account the initial fears, hostility, and confusion which will be present.* Most strategies are limited to what is going to be implemented and how. Explicit consideration of the time needed to get through the initial phase is usually never addressed. Time is needed to work with the individual affected by the change, to hear the individual's reactions, concerns, and questions, and to respond adequately as a necessary part of the change strategy. During these early stages, the focus is on understanding what is happening and on the problems of separating from the past. There is not yet a need to implement an action plan or fully embrace the new circumstances. Most of the activity will be internal as the individual begins to understand and slowly accept the need to change. The challenge for managers is to try to understand the process, allow it to happen, and if necessary, provide employees with assistance through careful listening, support, and opportunities to recognize the passing of the old.

3. *Choose the leaders of the implementation for their ability to deal with intangible, subjective, and ambiguous issues and feelings.* The leadership style usually preferred is best characterized by a take-charge, dynamic, aggres-

sive decision maker. We have frequently seen this sort of manager push for decisive action too soon. Their own drive for action pushes toward an early resolution of the many difficult implementation problems. They usually have little patience for the more subtle, less tangible issues of the early stages of change and cannot provide leadership for others who are attempting the difficult negotiation from the old to the new. If these issues are recognized at all by "action-oriented" managers, they usually respond by pressing harder for change and early resolution of ambiguous problems. It is difficult for them to recognize that it is not (necessarily) the goals of the change but the need to give up the old, familiar ways and cognitive maps of the existing organization in question.

4. Make managers aware of what is happening during the early stages of moving to action. Managers are not accustomed to handling the responses of their staff to the new, unsettling circumstances. A half-day session that presents the reactions to the implementation and the value of effective responses allows managers to examine their own experiences and reactions to major change. A deeper understanding of what is occurring will allow them to exercise more helpful and effective leadership. We caution not to try to give managers the tools or attitudes of therapists. It is neither necessary nor desirable. To respond adequately requires only an understanding of what is happening and an appreciation of the legitimacy of the many reactions of the staff to the changes. For most, listening, patience, consideration, and thoughtfulness will be a sufficient response. Most of us, as mature human beings, are quite capable of doing what is needed once we accept the need and importance of doing it.

5. Observe people's reactions to the implementation and create new opportunities for the abilities revealed and developed. Implementation of any strategy exposes people to new situations which may reveal strengths unseen until then. Watch for people who rise in response to the changes, deal with their own and others' reactions constructively, and formulate new solutions. Some will respond to the pressure for implementation as a problem to be avoided or fought. Others will see it as an opportunity for growth and will attempt to solve problems rather than be overwhelmed by difficult circumstances. Leadership ability will emerge, sometimes from surprising places, and opportunities should be quickly sought to develop future leaders. As the Chinese express it: "It is only during a storm, when the tree is uplifted, that you can see the depth of its roots."

ENERGIZE WITHOUT SCARING

Once employees are past the denial stage, it is time to move to action. As employees move to action, there is a fine line between excitement and despair. It is important to keep employees attuned to the urgency of the situation, but to continually bombard employees with information that competition is tough, costs are out of control, products are uncompetitive, the organization is not innovative, or it's crashing and burning will only lead to confusion and despair. The employees will translate urgency into purposeful action only if they have a sense of direction and if they think they have a fighting chance. They will translate urgency into inaction, despair, and defense of the status quo if they have no sense of direction and see the situation as hopeless. The nature of the situation does not determine whether people stay or flee. It is how they see the situation and what they think can be done. The message to managers is that communicating the urgency of the situation is important, but providing direction and the sense that success is within reach is essential. Employees must feel they can do something to influence what happens.

Focus on a Limited Number of Surmountable Factors

A natural human tendency is to identify others as the main source of problems. If only *they* could change. *They* are usually corporate staff, another unit in the organization, the board of directors, the competition, and government. Each level in the organization can point to someone above them or outside of the corporation that is the real problem. Of course they have very little control over whoever they have identified. So, why not recognize them as a constraint and focus on something you can change?

It is easy to become focused on overcoming uncontrollable constraints: the interest rates, the labor supply, technological development. If you truly have little probability of changing them, do not try. Define them as constraints and concentrate on working around them. In the long run you may be able to change some of the constraints you face, but do not grind to a halt waiting. Change what you can change and get on with it. Continuous short-run actions and improvements get us where we want to be in the long run. Pull to action by focusing on important, controllable factors.

Put People in the Inner Circle and Expect Involvement and Commitment

You can energize without scaring by giving people a role. Expect involvement and commitment. Jack McElwee, former president of John Hancock, tells an interesting story about turning a military unit around. He was in the Naval Air Reserve and took over as Commanding Officer of a fighter squadron. The unit was notorious for its malcontents and bad performance. Several of the key people did not want to be there. Many were just putting in their time. They showed up late and often were unprepared. Requests for transfers out were processed only as fast as regulations would permit. McElwee was given the unit as his first command. His opening discussion with the squadron members went something like this:[3]

> Hi, I am Jack McElwee . . . I'm complimented to have been assigned to this squadron with you . . . Scuttlebutt (Navy lingo for gossip, rumor) has it that some of you are not happy with this outfit and would like to get transferred. For this drill period I have suspended normal procedures for requesting transfers. On the table in the back you will find a stack of transfer requests. They are signed by me, all you have to do is fill in your name. You and I should not serve together if you don't want to . . . If you leave, I hope your next unit will be as good for you as this one will be in a short while . . . The rest is up to you. I only want to work with people who want to be here . . . and I suspect that really good people feel that way . . . together, we're going to show folks around here what a good squadron looks like. I hope most of you choose to stay. But you should decide to stay only if you can commit to the work and fun required to turn this into the best squadron on this station. If you have any questions, talk to me!! I'd like to have you with us, but I can understand if you can't make the commitment. To those of you who want to be part of a crack unit I'll see you next week, in uniform and on time.

There was a lot of discussion throughout the rest of the two-day drill period. Two men out of the 44 picked up forms on the way home. They sent them in and by the following week they were in new units. Forty-two men went home willing to risk that together they could make things work. Some even polished their boots, starched their uniforms and showed up the following week *on time.* Gradually they turned into the crack outfit they knew they could become. Notice particularly that it did not take any more time to be crack unit than it did to be the dregs. It took energy, focus, and involvement. McElwee gave them the energy by giving them responsibility and a focus on what they could become.

Once involved, employees become energized by feeling like they are part of that special group that makes things happen. We use the word *group* deliberately. To continue the military analogy, research has found that people do not throw themselves on hand grenades for God, mother, and country. They throw themselves on hand grenades for the small group trying to survive in a very hostile environment. Employees become energized by focusing on surmountable odds. They stay energized because of a commitment and involvement with their work group. They feel a part of their work group and part of that inner circle that makes things happen.

Even as President of John Hancock, Jack McElwee strived to make everyone feel part of the inner circle, the group making things happen. He accomplished this in part with his style. If you walked into his office, he

---

[3]Based on personal conversation, quoted with permission, 1992.

immediately sat on the couch and talked about the stuffed bear sitting in the chair, the airplane pictures on the wall, and the view of Boston from his office. If you had some association with the military he told you ex-military stories. If you had kids, he told you stories about his kids. Then it was time for business, hard-hitting business. You were brought in to his circle. He shared with you inside information and kept you up to date on what was happening. He made you feel like you were a trusted confidant. What is amazing about Jack McElwee is he did it with everyone. He did it with people coming into his office; he did it when he addressed small groups, and he did it when he spoke to the 1,500 managers of John Hancock in the Hancock Hall. They left feeling like they were part of the inside group making things happen.

Celebrate the Small Victories and Early Wins

People tire if they do not feel they are making progress. People need to feel something is happening, that they are being successful. Professional fund raisers utilize this logic extensively. One of the basic rules of fund raising is that a campaign should not be taken public until 50 percent of the money is already raised. People are much more likely to contribute if you tell them: "We are well on our way, but we need your help to get over the top." Call it the band-wagon effect or principle of momentum: Getting the thing moving is much more difficult than keeping it moving. The manager's job is to start the movement. All employees have to do is jump on and help keep it moving.

Of course, don't tell people something is moving when it is dead in the water. Always obtain the support of those most critical to the success of the endeavor—the boss, a supplier, a legislator—before making optimistic announcements. You do not want to be in the position of trying to get everyone on board when the most critical people are on the side lines.

Once the train starts moving, you can keep it moving by celebrating the early wins. In fact, it is best to design the program or project so a few early wins are guaranteed. Do not wait until the full objective is accomplished to celebrate. People will tire. They need encouragement and a sense that progress is being made along the way. Small celebrations let them know their efforts are paying off.

Make Sure Everyone Understands the Competition

Build a sense of action and urgency by making sure everyone understands the competition. Competitors are not standing still. In fact, now organizations face competitors which they have never faced before.

Consider the financial services industry. Historically loans were obtained from a bank, insurance from a life insurance firm, and stock from investment brokerages. Since the industry was deregulated in 1978, banks, insurance companies, and stock brokerage firms have become direct competitors, each able to offer services formerly the domain of the others. Firms in any one of these three industries now face competitors they have never faced before.

One way for a bank to give its employees an understanding of the competition would be to have them conduct a competitive analysis of, for example, Yamaichi Securities (Japanese investment bank), Salomon Brothers (U.S. investment bank), The Travelers (U.S. insurance company), and BankAmerica Corporation (U.S. bank). This may seem a bit radical, since marketing normally handles that type of research, but try it, keeping in mind the previous warning about the fine line between excitement and despair.

The purpose of competitive analysis is to familiarize your people with the actions of others. They should develop benchmarks of good practices against which to compare themselves. The competitive analysis does not have to be complicated but some general guidelines apply:

1. *Clearly focus the purpose of the competitive analysis.* Before people begin, identify a key problem, opportunity, or product on which to focus. Do not send them out with a general "find out how we are doing in relation to the competition" assignment. Make sure that the problem is relevant to the people conducting the analysis. For example, John Hancock recently revised its performance appraisal and compensation system. Part of the process of designing the new system was an analysis of performance appraisal systems in other companies. As another example, Flint Engineering, a unit of General Motors, conducted an analysis of how engineering units at IBM, GE, Hewlett-Packard and GMFanuc Robotics managed the engineering process. Involved were those from Flint charged with improving its engineering process.

2. *Visit other companies.* Competitive analysis should not be solely a number-crunching exercise. Consider all available statistical information, but more importantly, send people out to visit and interview as many other firms in the field as possible. Action and urgency will come from seeing what others are doing, not from looking at numbers. You will be surprised how open and willing others are to share. Of course they will keep their new product developments and marketing strategies to themselves, but they will provide you with a wealth of information. In many cases, it is also very useful to visit noncompetitors who share similar problems. Make the visits a two-way street. Give useful information in exchange for useful information. For example, visit four or five organizations and provide a summary report to all so everyone gains from the effort. Check with the companies in advance regarding how much disclosure they are comfortable with. Some may want their names identified with specific practices, while others prefer to remain anonymous.

3. *Visit customers and suppliers.* Customers and suppliers can be valuable sources of information about the competitive environment. This sounds like common sense, but amazingly it has been a long time since many managers have talked with a customer or a supplier. Involve managers and executives in customer service. Require that they serve on the hot lines, answering questions about the products or services. Have them visit suppliers to find out what is happening.

4. *Use competitors' products.* Most companies want managers to use exclusively their own products. In fact in some organizations it becomes an obsession. We recently had a discussion with a Vice-President of General Cinema Corporation, a large national distributor of Pepsi-Cola. He refuses to drink Coca-Cola. He said he breaks out in a rash just thinking about any other soft drink. General Motors managers drive and rent only GM cars. Gillette executives only use Right Guard. If your corporation has similar norms, you are missing a good opportunity to understand the competition. Drink their soft drinks, rent their cars, use their toothpaste, and do it as part of a continuous analysis of the competition.

5. *Do not become trapped in the "get me one of them" syndrome.* The risk you run when visiting competition is that from each product you test and each organization you visit you will select the most appealing aspect and "want it." The magic of a product is not only in the characteristics of any component but how the components fit together. You cannot construct a world-class vehicle by selecting from BMW the best brakes, from Ferrari the best design, from Volvo the best chassis, and from Honda the best exhaust system. BMW brakes don't work with Ferrari designs and Volvo chassis. You construct a world-class vehicle by deciding what type of vehicle you want and then carefully integrating compatible concepts and components.

6. *Include an analysis of process as well as product.* In a recent analysis we did of product development in major American firms for a large U.S. manufacturing company, an overriding conclusion was that more improvement in productivity would come from a focus on the management processes rather than from a focus on product. By management processes, we mean, for example, the methods by which products are designed, approvals given, funds appropriated, teams formed, decisions made, and information channeled and used. Management processes are as important to understand as the products produced.

Make everyone responsible for being competitive. Competitive analysis and taking the necessary action to be competitive should be part of everyone's job. Planning should include competitive analysis and actions. A proposal for a new product or service should include an analysis of competitive products. Decisions about new production processes should include a competitive analysis. Wage and salary decisions should be based on competitive analysis. In short, part of everyone's responsibility should be understanding how they compare to others outside of the organization, and to take action to ensure competitiveness.

Some organizations keep executives up to date by displaying data concerning how they are doing relative to competition in so-called "war rooms." They pick selected factors and track the data over time. For example, market penetration, return rate, and customer opinion measures are useful comparisons with readily available data in many industries. Industry and professional associations also collect reams of comparative data from many companies on everything from salaries to investment in facilities. The key, of course, is to focus on the critical variables and track the progress of the action plan put in place to achieve the goal.

MAKE PURPOSEFUL ACTION
A MANAGEMENT PRIORITY

Many organizations are currently emphasizing participation, delegation, and various other organization development (OD) techniques. All of these can make tremendous contributions, but they are matters of style and by themselves do not guarantee action.

We have seen this point demonstrated very clearly. A large corporation we worked with centralized some of its divisions into product groups. The organization of these groups is basically the same. A very strong-willed vice-president, who believed strong, centralized leadership would make the difference between success and failure, was placed at the head of one group. Not a manager to emphasize participation, he defined a few goals and focused his time and energy on implementing them. He worked hard to make sure he made good, solid, business decisions.

The vice-president in charge of the other group emphasized participation and delegation. A much more democratic leader, he believed in a bottom-up approach to goal setting. His focus was on promoting an atmosphere of participation and teamwork. After 18 months, each group vice-president asked us to report on progress in their respective groups.

After conducting hundreds of interviews across all functions and levels in each group, we found vast differences between the two but one striking similarity: Neither group was moving to action. The first group had a clear sense of purpose and goals, but they were spending all their time conducting analyses and feeding information up the hierarchy. They were waiting for someone to tell them what to do. They did not feel involved or responsible for what was happening.

The second group was also frustrated with the lack of progress. They expressed disappointment and made comments like, "We're floundering . . . we are nowhere near where I had expected." They were tired of the continuous round of off-sites, team-building, and planning sessions. They wanted to agree on a set of goals and get on with it.

Feedback of the results to each group vice-president brought swift, effective action. The first vice-president assigned responsibility for implementation. He called a halt to the analysis and focused the organization on producing results. The other vice-president took even more dramatic action, setting clear business objectives, pulling his top management together for a day to discuss the need for action and results, and then visiting every unit and plant in his division to communicate and reinforce the newly articulated set of business objectives. He changed the agenda of his regular staff meetings to a review of each unit's progress with respect to their goals. He focused the off-site and group sessions on implementation.

The first vice-president remained an autocratic leader, but now he was emphasizing results rather than analysis. The second vice-president retained his participative style but now he was expecting action and results. The style differences between the two are not what made the difference, the call to action is.[4]

Promote Risk Taking

One of the effective ways to build a sense of action and urgency on the part of the employees in the company is to encourage taking risks. The fear of failure is the reason risks aren't taken. Employees think that their bosses will not tolerate the errors that are inherent in trying new things. We've talked about the reward system and other policies and procedures that need to be examined in order to support risk taking and encourage taking the initiative. But the best way for leaders to convey the message that a sense of action and urgency is desired is to display it themselves.

For example, Frederick Smith set a tone of action and initiative taking in Federal Express when he founded the company in the early 1970s. A former Marine Corps officer, Smith risked millions of dollars in starting up an overnight-air delivery service. He built the company in 1988 to revenues of $3.99 billion, based on his initial risk taking and his continual risk and initiative taking throughout the years. Not all his ventures have succeeded. When ZAPMAIL AM failed miserably in 1984, he lost a lot of money. But it served as a testimonial to his employees that the worst thing to fear was the fear of failure.

MANAGER'S CHECKLIST

1. Have each department include in their strategy explanations how their action will help other units implement their strategy. Have departments identify those units within the organization with which they

---

work most closely and have them jointly submit plans for improving customer value.

2. Require all staff advisors to submit action plans and implementation schedules with their recommendations. Whenever possible assign staff advisors to implementation teams.

3. Build time into your implementation plans to deal with denial and resistance. Create forums for people to share with you their anger and frustration with changes. Before you talk with them, make a list of reactions you would feel if you were in their situation.

4. Include in your list of criteria for promotional decisions such action and urgency criteria as helping people learn from failure, listening to criticism, helping people deal with the frustrations of change, being able to counsel troubled employees, showing employees how to improve performance, and so on.

5. Focus, focus, focus. The magic of successful management is focusing on controllable factors that can make significant differences. You must be more than heat transfer, passing on the multiple requests you get from other parts of the organization to your subordinates. Prioritize them and pass on only the critical few that will deliver maximum payoff.

6. Develop competitive benchmarks for your own job. Establish mechanisms for keeping up to date with others doing your type of job in other organizations; join professional groups, attend user conferences, visit competitors and clients, keep up to date.

CHAPTER 7

Key #5: Continuously Adapt and Improve

*A*fter communicating the strategy, positioning your key performers, unleashing the potential of your employees, and building the excitement, you may be tempted to sit back and watch the results of your work. After all, delegation means turning responsibility over to employees and letting them perform. The plans are in place, the resources properly allocated, and people assigned to correct positions. You have done your job, now it is someone else's turn to implement the changes. Unfortunately, there will be no rest. The simple fact is that you will not get it right the first time, you must continuously move people to action. Your purpose is not to implement the changes. Your purpose is to continuously change, adapt, and improve. Not because you have not given it your best efforts, but because the situation changes and the game is never over.

THE SITUATION IS UNPREDICTABLE

Most managers cry out for stability. They want predictability. They view their job in a linear fashion—one crisis at a time. They feel comfortable identifying a critical problem, determining a solution, managing the implementation process, and then moving on to the next problem. Of course, customer preferences change, competition makes advances and adjustments, and technology changes. In addition, the organization shifts. Systems do not work quite the expected way. New ideas are discovered. Plans are never perfectly implemented. Neither horse races nor business competitions are won by those who get off to a fast start and rigidly follow a predetermined plan to the end. Good strategic managers get good starts, have a general strategy, and monitor and respond quickly to events along the way. They continuously adapt and improve. They accept as a fact of life that any change brings the need for more changes, some of which cannot be anticipated. Following are some examples.

Managing Negative Reactions

A multibillion dollar manufacturer of chemicals streamlined operations and focused on traditional areas of strength. A significant reorganization was carried out to help implement the new strategy.

With several divisions being consolidated, hundreds of people had to move to new locations. While the placement and movement of people were carefully managed, the sheer number of moves resulted in employees viewing the new strategy as ill-conceived and chaotic. By monitoring employee reactions, management picked up this sentiment.

Management immediately recognized the need to deal with the employees' reactions and considered doing so as the company's opportunity to reaffirm its concern for employees. Rather than just addressing the issue of relocating jobs, the top management group addressed the importance of the employees in every aspect of the business. They examined compensation, training, and appraisal systems to ensure they were up to date and consistent with the new strategy. Managers who had pushed decision making downward were recognized in a day-long program. Bonuses for people-oriented accomplishments were established. The group implemented diagonal staff meetings so managers on all levels could continuously monitor progress. They never hesitated to make adjustments to programs and systems that were not working as anticipated.

Managing Overreactions

In another company, monitoring showed that too few resources were being directed at customers in the very profitable, older segment of the market. The newer markets were more exciting and managers were overallocating their sales power to them rather than servicing older markets. The organization was pulled too far away from profitable, older markets. Through a careful monitoring by internal staff, this was spotted before it became a serious problem. Resources were reallocated back to markets which, though less exciting, were solid and profitable.

THE GAME IS NEVER OVER

In 1985, business publications such as *The Wall Street Journal*, *Business Week*, and *Fortune* announced that IBM had won the personal computer war. The IBM PC had clearly outpaced comparable products from Apple Computer, Digital Equipment, Hewlett-Packard, and several other top-ranked computer firms. The analogy to winning the war had two fallacies. First, wars are won by beating the opponent. After a certain number of critical battles the enemy admits defeat and surrenders. Who wins is determined by who loses. Unlike war, the sole purpose of business cannot be beating the competition. If you focus on beating a certain number of other businesses, the best you can do is a little better than the others. Focusing on winning as the sole driving force for what you do substantially limits what you can accomplish. You will never achieve the big breakthroughs, the critical innovations, or the organizational transformations necessary to truly be a leader. You will never establish the critical linkages with suppliers and cooperative relationships with other organizations necessary to survive.

The purpose of business is to create value and serve multiple stakeholders: customers, stockholders, employees, and society in general. Competition is merely an artifact of our economic system, a way we have decided to play the game. Undoubtedly for us, it is a very valuable artifact. It provides motivation and, over time, eliminates most of those who do not provide value. But if it becomes the total focus, the customer gradually loses. The combatants become so involved in beating each other, they forget their true purpose is to deliver value.

The second fallacy of the analogy to war is that it is in everyone's interest that wars end. But competition need not have an ending. The competition to deliver value to computer users is not over. As IBM has discovered since 1985, no one has a guaranteed market share and a product that solves all customers' problems. In reality, customers really do not want precisely your products. They have needs and are looking for products and services that fit those needs. If yours happens to come closest in comparison to all available at the moment, customers will buy it. But if they find something else that meets their needs later, they will switch even if the substituted product does not resemble yours. In personal computers some unknown may suddenly develop a "killer technology," something that renders all other products obsolete. Someone may suddenly announce a voice-activated, artificial intelligence system which looks and works more like a tape recorder than a computer. Customers may like it because their need is for hard-copy communication. They really do not care how it gets from their head onto a piece of paper.

In business you can never sit back and say, the war is over and we won. You can never stop improving. It is not a war and it is never over. Xerox in the 1960s and 1970s had a very dominant market share. They kept pushing their line and developing even more sophisticated large-volume copiers. By all appearances, they had won. They dominated technologically and in the market. However, Ricoh and Savin did not receive word that the war was over. They developed technology aimed at the low end of the markets: personal and small business copiers. They used this as a wedge and gradually destroyed Xerox's market leadership. Xerox has had to work long and hard to regain its market leadership.

Similarly, General Motors once commanded 60 percent of the automobile market. Chevrolet alone held nearly one third of the market. Government officials once considered antitrust legislation to break up the giant and prevent a monopoly. But foreign competition and the oil crisis did the job for them. In 1992, General Motors held less than 35 percent of the market share, Chevrolet less than 15 percent, and General Motors continues to lose ground. For General Motors, a new game has begun.

BUILD A DRIVE
FOR CONTINUOUS IMPROVEMENT

What we are suggesting is that you are never done. Your people have to keep in contact with what is happening at all times. What you need from your people is a willingness to aggressively pursue good business risks, an ability to monitor themselves and quickly adjust, and a determination to continually improve. Fine tuning as you go is the key to success. People must be committed to continuous improvement.

Let's look at how one company's fine tuning and continuous improvement was necessary to implement a major new strategy. When Keith Crane was appointed chief executive officer of Colgate-Palmolive he developed a plan to turn around the faltering consumer packaged-goods company. A decade of acquisitions activity in a dozen or so areas including cosmetics and sporting goods had weakened the company's profit performance and detracted attention from its core soap and toothpaste products. Quality and consumer acceptance of the products dropped. Colgate-Palmolive's stock had foundered for years and Wall Street saw little in the picture to cheer about. Meanwhile, Procter & Gamble had begun an orderly and powerful European expansion program threatening markets historically dominated by Colgate, especially aimed at their core brands. Colgate needed to refocus on its core businesses and become profitable again.

Crane's plan involved:

1. The immediate sell-off of unprofitable and unrelated businesses. The cash would be used to "reinvest" in the core product lines.
2. A strategy of "Product Health" which meant rebuilding product quality, advertising excellence, and capital programs in support of the core soap, detergent, and toothpaste brands.
3. A global approach to organization, replacing the historical domestic and international divisions. The corporation would be structured and managed by focusing on product lines rather than geographic divisions.
4. The establishment of a powerful, corporate Business Development Group responsible for coordinating development across the business units.

5. The needed investments would continue to be made until the problems were fixed and "Product Health" was achieved. Although profits would be considered of secondary importance initially, they would come as the natural result of doing the right things.

The plan was communicated forcefully by Crane. He took every opportunity to reinforce it, as did his key executives. However, the process of implementing the plan was anything but smooth. Using an extensive monitoring system, Crane identified numerous problems along the way and each was resolved in turn resulting in a fine tuning of the basic organization they had in place.

The first surprise was how much effort was needed to adapt the old management information and budgeting systems so that they could monitor not only revenues and expenditures, but quality, market share, customer satisfaction, and other factors needed to implement the new strategy. The Systems Department could not handle the additional work load required to fix the information systems. To resolve the problem, Crane hired more people to deal with the increased workload.

Once the information and budgeting systems were fixed, problems were discovered with the billing and credit systems. They were not set up by product line, but rather by geographical area. Requiring major modifications, this impeded the efforts of the Systems Department. The solution to this problem was to revise billing and credit systems gradually, rather than all at once. Over a three-month period of time, 100 departments changed their billing and crediting systems to reflect the new focus on product lines.

Another unanticipated change was required in the compensation system. It did not adequately recognize and reward the behavior consistent with the new strategy. Managers were reviewing the appropriate information by product line and had billing and credit systems that supported the strategy, but the compensation system was still focused on Colgate's general business performance rather than on the performance of the individual product lines. Through monitoring, Crane and his staff caught the inconsistency and a new compensation system was developed.

Monitoring also revealed that the extensive restructuring and redesigning had put significant pressure on managers. Managers needed to free themselves up by delegating more. But they could only do this if their employees developed skills to cope with major changes. Managers also had to master new processes of decision making and communication, each of which required new skills. In response, Colgate implemented a "Managing Change" workshop that was attended by all of its managers. The one-week workshop included training on how to use feedback mechanisms to measure progress and how to focus on continuous improvement.

It took three years of fine tuning along the way before the new systems and structure were operating smoothly. Hindsight is twenty-twenty.

It is easy to see things after the fact that should have been anticipated. Looking forward it is impossible to predict everything. The best we can do is take our best shot, learn along the way, and improve as we go. Monitoring is the key to making continuous improvement a reality. Employees must have information about their progress and must be responsible for using this information to improve their performance.

WHY DOESN'T MONITORING OCCUR?

Even though monitoring is so critical, people often resist doing it because it takes time and often involves the delivery of bad news. The best monitoring can do is indicate that work is on track and progress should continue as is. The worst it can do is indicate you are off track and must change. The problem, of course, is the tendency to regard the need to change as failure—you blew it; you did not get it right; your analysis was faulty, your plans incomplete, or your implementation not managed correctly. In truth, the need to revise plans often reflects more on the complex and dynamic world we live in.

Compounding the problem, techniques used to measure strategic progress are often rudimentary at best. Most questionnaires and surveys are too complex and not specifically focused on strategy; thus, they do not provide data that help organizations to respond. Interviews are excellent sources of data but they take more time and energy than the other methods, and often more time and energy than the organization can feasibly spend on the issue at hand. Accounting and budget systems that use financial data are often too aggregated and are not relevant to individual workers trying to improve their production performance. The forces working against monitoring often prevail. Therefore, people do not always have the data they need to improve their performance.

Resistance to monitoring can be countered. First, managers and employees can be trained to track their own progress. Second, any flagging of problems should not be dealt with by "shooting the messenger." Rather, it should be viewed as an opportunity to learn and correct. As Edwin Land, the founder of Polaroid, said, "A mistake is only something we have yet to learn from."

What Should Be Monitored?

Traditional information systems alone will probably not provide managers with all the data they need. Traditional systems focus on such factors as economic and numeric goals, budgets, production schedules, scrap, capital investment, and return on expenditures. Though these are all important, they do not provide sufficient information to allow managers to monitor total strategic progress. Managers also need information about the people side of the business. How motivated are employees to implement strategy?

How well do they understand the strategy? How committed are they to making it work?

Two categories of information are necessary:

1. *Task Data.* These data are often seen as hard measures. They are usually quantifiable and relate to economic and market results. Examples are units of production per person, reject rates, costs of production per unit, sales and profits.

2. *People Data.* These are data on attitudes, commitment, coordination effectiveness, and team effectiveness. These softer measures are often more difficult to quantify. They are, however, essential because they provide data on the state of the human organization.

For example, after a major reorganization managers in the Chevrolet Central Office developed a monitoring system to monitor both sets of data. They instituted a system to identify how well the reorganization and their strategy of regaining market share were taking hold. Along with "outcome" objectives on market share, productivity, and quality, they included "people" objectives in their five-year business plan.

- Communicate a Chevrolet vision, mission, and strategic direction to all employees so that they understand and become committed.
- Shift the Chevrolet focus from "organization" to "team," and from "departments" to "teamwork."
- Improve the overall quality, capability, and promotability of Chevrolet employees through education, training, and cross-functional experience.

Progress on these softer goals was reported quarterly by using a "Strategy Action Questionnaire" specifically focusing on these areas. Also, a sample of 30 people was selected from across all functions and levels at the Central Office and interviewed quarterly to indicate individuals' reactions to the changes. The results of the interviews were summarized and reported to senior management along with recommendations for action. Based on the assessment, the following actions were taken:

1. A Management Information Conference was held to communicate the Chevrolet mission and objectives to all management.

2. Videotapes were sent monthly to update all employees on progress and events within Chevrolet.

3. The education program was revised to focus more on the communication and understanding of Chevrolet's mission and business plan.

4. Task forces were established to coordinate efforts across functions.

The need for these actions was apparent from the quarterly assessments. The quantitative market penetration results could not have revealed the need for more communication about the business plan, nor the need to revise the education program, nor the value of task forces cutting across functional lines. The quarterly interviews also identified the need for the actions months before the harder data would have revealed any problems whatsoever. The monitoring of "people" goals was effective because it revealed important information about the people responsible for accomplishing the strategy.

Using Monitoring to Drive Continuous Improvement

Once data are collected, they must be used to drive continuous improvement. Collecting data is simple in comparison to getting people to use the information to improve their performance. Following are suggestions which greatly increase the probabilities that data will be used to effectively drive continuous improvement.

1. *Make the data directly relevant to employees' responsibilities.* The best plants, ranging in industries from paper making to automotive to computers to chemicals, have all workers identify the information they need to monitor their own progress and establish procedures and systems to collect it. The plant manager's job is to help the people get the data. The employees' responsibility is to set goals, measure their own performance, adjust and improve.

2. *Monitor and present critical issues succinctly and clearly.* In one corporation we studied, a competently executed questionnaire produced reams of data about employees' attitudes toward management, major business goals, and organization. The data were analyzed in terms of the respondent's department, level in the organization, and age. Three-dimensional plots were made to present the data. The result of this extensive effort and presentation was not action, only a polite "thank you" from the managers who received it. The issues that management needed to deal with were lost in the data. At the same time, another group collected data through interviews. They interviewed 50 people, rather than the thousands who had filled out the questionnaire. Their feedback to management was organized in terms of the goals management had articulated for the organization. The data were summarized in crisp, succinct sentences such as:

   - "There is confusion about target markets. We are wasting resources fighting internally."
   - "We are spending way too much time off site talking about organization and management. We are wasting time. We need to get back to the product."

Seven or eight of these highlights with supporting quotes were the whole of the feedback. Following the quotes were two or three suggested actions that could be taken immediately to resolve the problems.

- "Hold people accountable for focusing on specific market segments; be sure resources are allocated consistently with this strategy."
- "Change the agenda of senior staff meetings to focus on products and pushing business results."

The same management team that could muster only polite thanks to the feedback from the elaborate questionnaire responded to the feedback from the interviews by implementing several key actions. The pictures painted by both surveys were the same, the problems they revealed identical. The difference was the immediately perceived relevance of the second, the ease with which it could be understood, and the clarity of the actions suggested. Presentation of data was the goal of the first group. Action and continuous improvement were the goals of the second group.

3. *Aim at the right level.* For information to be useful it must go to the people who have the power to act on it. If information goes to a level above where it is needed, then employees feel managers are looking over their shoulders. The game is no longer monitoring and improving—it is justifying yourself to the boss. If information goes to a level below where it is needed, the employee who needs it never gets it and is powerless to act. Information concerning whether defects are high, turnover is high, or attitudes are not positive must go to decision makers who can do something about these problems. Managers must be able to take ownership of the problem and take action. If relevant data do not go to the decision makers who can use them, nothing will get done.

A Case Study: Beta Engineering

The implications of continuously adapting and improving are most clearly understood in the context of a real example. We chose an organizational change example to show how continuously monitoring and adapting to people or the soft side of business is so important. The organizational change itself was the subject of continuous improvement. Recently Beta Engineering (a fictitious name), a manufacturer of complex equipment for the telephone industry, underwent a major organizational change in response to increasing overseas competition and changes in the purchasing strategy of its major customers. Previously, the firm was organized by function with the heads of Research, Development, Planning, Production, Sales, and other groups reporting to the president. The new structure was organized around programs targeted at major market segments and resources allocated to do business in each segment located under a vice-president. Each vice-president had profit and loss responsibility.

The president personally announced the new organizational structure and followed the announcement with an extensive (and exhaustive) round of meetings with each unit to get feedback from the organization. These were followed by "diagonal" slice meetings where representatives from all levels and departments within the unit were introduced to the new organization by the president and further revisions suggested. Since the president personally and repeatedly outlined the major organizational changes and the need to work out the details, the issue was moved quickly from a "grand design" handed down by top management to a new set of organizational arrangements all were expected to review and improve.

Beta Engineering involved employees using diagonal slice teams in a detailed study of the company's competitive industry position. This included comparisons with competitor's products, cost-efficiency measures, quality levels, and forecasts of future strategies. The results were startling. Each team came away from the study with a clear and alarming view of the company's competitive disadvantage. From this work, each unit analyzed its own strengths and weaknesses which led to a more detailed understanding of how the competition had beaten Beta Engineering in a number of key areas. This led to a widespread understanding that the further changes needed were neither cosmetic nor limited to a few ineffective managers. Most staff involved in the process were ready and eager to implement the serious corrective action required to improve their performance.

Detailed operational plans requiring a range of further changes from substantial reorganization to a change in the method of payment to suppliers were developed. Although these plans had to be approved by the president, the planning effort was so thorough that 60 percent of all employees participated in some part of the process. They were invested in the changes and determined to make them work.

The communications mechanisms initiated by the president at the start of the process were kept active providing feedback on how well implementation was going and what additional refinements were needed. Constant monitoring and adjustment allowed the reorganization to go smoothly. The president demonstrated a willingness to quickly adopt further improvements consistent with the strategy and structure of reorganization. The attitude of continual improvement was finally established.

Manager's Checklist

1. Each month take an hour and analyze your own work habits. Develop a list of ways you can improve. Make one of your work habits taking time to continuously improve.

2. Monitoring is the key to continuous improvement. Put in place tracking mechanisms that will allow you to monitor your own work activ-

ities and results. Find a trusted friend you can sit down with once a month and talk through your successes and failures.

3. In your monitoring systems make sure you include both task and people information.

4. Never accept the answer, "If it is not broken, don't fix it." Everything can be improved and should be subject to evaluation and improvement. A better way always exists.

CHAPTER 8

The Beginning

DIRECTING STRATEGY:
THE BEGINNING

R eading this book we hope your reaction so far is that these keys seem fairly straightforward. We do not offer programs or complicated procedures requiring studies or expensive consultants. We have attempted to offer simple, common-sense advice. Why? Because wherever we have seen effective management and leadership, it has been done in a simple, uncomplicated manner. The keys offered do not require any further elaboration; the time for discussion is past. The time for acting has arrived.

At the end of our book we would like to take a brief moment to talk about the beginning, the beginning of putting the keys to high performance into practice. You may have many reasons why you cannot act. The most common reason we hear is that you lack approvals. Many activities to implement these keys do not need approvals. You do not need approvals for making sure communication is clear and abundant up, down, and across the organization. You do not need approvals to remove barriers and get people excited about their work. You do not need approvals to help people understand the competition, the customer, and the changing world we all face.

Another reason for not acting is that you are not sure what to do first. Our response is do whatever seems to make the most sense. Do what feels right in your situation. Do what you can do. Do what will have the most impact. Do what will make a difference to you and your people, but most importantly, do *something*. Get on with it and make adjustments along the way. You will learn by trying.

Begin Where You Have the Most Influence

Begin where you can have the most influence. You have a lot to say about how much you communicate with others; begin there. You probably greatly influence how your employees spend their time and focus their energy. Begin there. Begin by making sure people understand what the words *strategy*, *objectives*, *teamwork*, and *development* mean. Begin by recognizing managers who work to develop their employees. Begin by rewarding small victories, by having little celebrations, by taking employees out to lunch to let them know you recognize their accomplishments. Begin by looking at what competition is doing to build a sense of action and urgency. Begin by acknowledging the feelings of your employees and by listening to their problems and complaints. Begin by passing on information, sharing what you know about what is happening in the organization and the environment. You control all of these areas. But most of all you control yourself. Begin with yourself.

Begin With Yourself

Very often middle managers identify top managers as their main constraints. If only they would change. Top managers, in turn, identify the president as their main constraint. We could implement the principles if only the president would change. The president identifies middle management as his or her main problem. If only they would change. Everyone points at someone else rather than accepting personal responsibility for making a difference. Do not worry about changing other people—change yourself. You have much more control over what you do than what they do. Change the way you manage and they will change how they work with you. You affect their behavior.

We have found one critical area you can affect that needs improvement so desperately in most organizations that it is worth your special attention—meetings. You have heard managers throughout organizations complain how much they dislike meetings. The response is, like it or not, that is how managers get things done. You have to work with people. The further up the organizational hierarchy you go, the more time you will spend in meetings and the more you will control what happens in those meetings. We often ask executives and managers to rate the usefulness of the meetings they attend. The average hovers around 70 percent worthless, 30 percent useful. What a waste of time and energy. Surprisingly, we get about the same ratings no matter what level in the organization we ask. Would people attending your meetings rate them 70 percent worthless? Probably! Start there. Start by assuming responsibility for using those meetings to implement these principles. Start by critically evaluating your meetings and eliminating those which are not useful. See that the objectives are clearly communicated, that people listen to each other, that the definitions of words are commonly understood, that the right people are present, that agendas are set and followed, and that there is a sense of action and urgency.

Stick With It

Our keys describe a new way of working with others, but do not expect miracles—at least not immediately. Change will occur slowly. Do not get discouraged if results are not immediate. Effective managers know change takes time. Jack Welch of General Electric speaks of change taking many years even for GE's smaller businesses.

Destruction can occur overnight; creation, change, and evolution take time and patience. By nature most managers are impatient, wanting and expecting immediate results. You need to set realistic expectations about the rate of change. Map out a step-by-step plan and stay on course. Do not get caught in what one manager referred to as "strategy du jour." You do not like the strategy management is setting? No problem, by tomorrow there will be a new one. If there is one thing that marks those who successfully act strategy, it is their dogged sense of purpose, commitment to keep going, and understanding that it takes time. They are best described as managing by "nudging." A push here, a pull there, constant pressure for improvement, steady gains, excitement about progress, and a constant eye on the ball. They do not let every bump in the road cause them to shift course wildly. Sure they make adjustments along the way, and sometimes they even change the script, but everything has its purpose and they are not making constant swings.

GMFanuc Robotics has seen its business fortunes rise and fall depending on industrial capital equipment expenditures. A slight slowing of the economy causes a significant downturn in orders for robots. They are in a business characterized by boom or bust, fluctuations over which they have little control. Rather than react to each fluctuation, Eric Mittelstadt, the president, and the executive group at GMFanuc Robotics have developed a five-year plan. Their five-year plan is quite different than most five-year plans we have seen because they use theirs. The main question the top management group asks is not "Did we meet the ten-day sales forecast?" but "Are we generally on track for our five-year plan?"

John Buono, President of Analytical Answers, coped with the need to develop a longer-term focus by adopting what he referred to as the "six-month rule." Changes take six months before they will show results. Make adjustments as you go, but wait six months before judging a change. Some changes take even longer than six months to have an impact.

One area where most managers are far too impatient is restructuring. We have been taught for a long time that "structure follows strategy." A new strategy requires a new structure. Because we do not have a very clear sense of strategy, something we can identify and stick with, we are always modifying, adapting, and changing the strategy. Hence, we have to continually change the structure, searching for the best way to organize.

Changing structure is a seductive managerial activity, it makes us feel like we have accomplished something. We can look at the boxes and lines and see change. Surely we must be making progress.

In general, the complete results of a reorganization will not be felt for three years. The first year people are recovering from the shock, getting the new phone directory, finding out whom they work with and report to, and reestablishing the informal network that allows the organization to function. The informal network is what makes the organization work, not the formal structure. The informal network is destroyed by reorganization and takes a year or more to establish. The second year people begin figuring out how to work and coordinate with others effectively. They begin performing. They have adjusted and fine tuned the organization so they can perform on a consistent basis by the third year.

Of course, this means that if you have major reorganizations every year, people never do get to the point where they can perform. Be a little slower to reorganize. You may be able to recover from a reorganization in less than three years, but you surely will not be able to do it in less than one year, which unfortunately is about the average length of time a structure lasts in some organizations today. The magic is not in the structure anyway. It is in the performance and that performance is delivered by people interacting with each other. People motivated to perform can learn how to make any structure work, but it takes time.

You need to set realistic time frames and realize not everything will happen at once. Draw out a flow chart of the implementation process. Identify what happens first and what happens next. Show how the changes relate to each other, and then keep track of your progress. Expect results, but realize you are in it for the long haul. Stick with it and make it work.

Unlearn and Learn

Kurt Lewin, many years ago, proposed a paradigm of:

UNFREEZING → CHANGE → REFREEZING

By unfreezing he meant getting people to accept the need for change. Then they change and refreeze the new behaviors in place. We believe that in the fluid, dynamic world we face, freezing is the wrong analogy. Nothing is ever stable enough to be frozen in place. A constant pressure exists for setting new objectives and discovering new ways to obtain these objectives. Rather than freezing and unfreezing, we find it useful to speak of constant unlearning and learning. Not only do you have to learn new ways of behaving, but you also have to unlearn the old ways.

The importance of unlearning is demonstrated by the Headstart Program, begun by the government in the 1960s. The Headstart Program focused on improving the basic skills of children before they entered kindergarten. Children were taken out of the home environment and given wonderful educational and training opportunities. Two decades later, the general consensus is that the program works best in situations when others from the child's home are involved. If children receive no encouragement or support from those at home to retain and use their new skills, they are rarely retained. If parents expect the old behaviors, that is what they will receive.

Management training programs are often great learning experiences for participants. They make new friends, develop new skills, and acquire many useful management tools. Then what happens? They go back to work where nothing has changed. Bosses still have the same demands, systems still work the same, work pressures remain the same. Even if they wanted to, they would find it very hard to use the skills and tools they have acquired. They cannot stop reverting back to their old behaviors. They cannot unlearn. They have to stop before they can start and the organization will not let them stop.

You need to consciously and aggressively manage the expectations others have of you. Point out why you are changing and what you expect to accomplish. Do not let actions speak for themselves. Actions are critical, but everyone will have a different interpretation of what you are doing. They will not let you change, they want you back the way you were. At least then you were predictable. Tell people what you are doing and why. Most importantly, tell them what you are *not* doing and why. Create your own opportunities to unlearn.

When John Buono decided he needed more time to spend on planning, customer contact, and working with top management, he started pushing decision making down. His staff had two reactions. First, "What is he doing to us now?" and second, "If we are doing all his work, what is he doing?" Their work together was very confusing until Buono explained to his staff how he was trying to change the way he managed. He needed to spend more time managing the total organization. He needed to delegate operational decisions downward and get more involvement from those in the organization that were closer to the action. All fine-sounding words, but it was not until Buono specifically detailed the types of decisions they would and would not be making that the staff began to understand. You have to tell people what you are *not* doing, as well as what you *are* doing.

Expect Success

A final word. You do not get up in the morning, look in the mirror and say, I think I will go out and fail today. Nobody does. Those who work for you want to succeed just as much as you do. It would be inconsistent with the philosophy of this book to approach directing strategy from any perspective other than expecting success. People will do what you expect them to do. If they start naturally wanting to succeed and end up failing, something along the way causes them to fail. That something is usually not a big catastrophic event. It is a series of small mistakes, barriers, and bad decisions that cumulatively get people off track. You will help get them back on track by expecting success. They will become what you expect them to be. Of course, you will have setbacks and problems—life does not come any other way. But, over the long haul, if you are clear about wanting to accomplish something really important and committed to helping other people help you, you will succeed. We wish you skill in your endeavors, for in reality luck has very little to do with success. You make your own luck.

It has been fun sharing our experiences with you. We have tried to provide you with ideas that can help you to be more productive. But in the final analysis, it is up to you. These recommendations are only as good as you utilize them in performance. We hope you will find them helpful, and use them.